"If there's one thing we can all learn from hackers, it's that you need to continually rethink your assumptions. Just like how hackers do this to improve the security of software systems, *Data Leadership for Everyone* helps you rethink your approach to data. This book helps demystify how to turn data from a misunderstood liability into a powerful asset. The author keeps the concepts accessible for both leaders and technologists, and everyone in between."

—Ted Harrington, #1 bestselling author of *Hackable* and leader of ethical hackers

"Anthony Algmin has never pulled any punches. Algmin's new book, *Data Leadership for Everyone*, starts with hard facts about what is wrong with Data Leadership today and quickly delves into what should be done to improve the situation. His Data Leadership Framework flawlessly explains a handful of actionable categories broken into pragmatic disciplines that direct you toward improved Data Leadership practices. This book will prepare you to start working and put Data Leadership into action."

—Robert S. Seiner, president/principal of KIK Consulting & Educational Services

"Clear, straightforward and with some humor injected, too, Anthony's writing style keeps the reader engaged at all times. For practitioners or leaders alike, this is a valuable resource that puts the vast world of data and data leadership in perspective and relatable terms for all!"

—Dora Boussias, transformational leader and data digital architecture

"Sometimes leadership of organizations need to learn new things. The tried-and-true capabilities of managing, planning, and budgeting are all covered and imbedded in business leader training—but these topics do not cover the new requirement that organization leaders must manage the data resource with the same intensity as capital, human resources, or inventory. This is what *Data Leadership for Everyone* is about. It offers a much-needed primer to assist management in engaging with the data resource. Anthony fills a huge gap in what leadership should know, versus what they currently know. Middle managers need to get very cozy with this book."

—John Ladley, author

DATA
LEADERSHIP
FOR EVERYONE

DATA
LEADERSHIP
FOR EVERYONE

HOW YOU CAN HARNESS THE TRUE POWER OF DATA AT WORK

ANTHONY J. ALGMIN

sourcebooks

This publication is designed to provide accurate and authoritative information in regard
to the subject matter covered. It is sold with the understanding that the publisher is not
engaged in rendering legal, accounting, or other professional service. If legal advice
or other expert assistance is required, the services of a competent professional person
should be sought.
—*From a Declaration of Principles Jointly Adopted by a Committee of the*
American Bar Association and a Committee of Publishers and Associations

Published by Sourcebooks
P.O. Box 4410, Naperville, Illinois 60567–4410
(630) 961-3900
sourcebooks.com

Cataloging-in-Publication Data is on file with the Library of Congress.

Printed and bound in the United States of America.
VP 10 9 8 7 6 5 4 3 2 1

For those compelled to make it better.

CONTENTS

Part 3: Data Leadership in Action

FOREWORD

Data in action. That is today's business goal. In this book, Anthony Algmin, a leading voice in data leadership and data-powered business strategy, cogently lays out the steps to give data its transformative power in the modern business environment. In ways both practical and elegant, the author convincingly demonstrates that putting data in action requires putting data leadership in action. This, in turn, requires learning the power of people as well as the power of data. It requires the professional skills to assess situations accurately, to determine the actions required based on those assessments, and to implement the actions—to put data in action—in a way that drives meaningful change and achieves business goals. The "data leadership framework" that Anthony developed and explains in this book is not just a theoretical framework, it also provides a toolkit to put data into action, which is what drives results. Whether you are a seasoned data professional, a business leader, an executive project sponsor, a data lawyer like me, or new to the field, this book provides the foundational understanding of data as a business asset and a practical guide to using that asset to achieve outcomes that matter.

In my years of working with Anthony, he has emphasized to me that data is defined by how it is used, that its meaningfulness and usefulness depend on its business context, that its value is derived from its context, and that as the context changes so does its meaningfulness and usefulness. This takes us back to the core of his data leadership framework: assess, determine actions, and implement them. In similar fashion, data turns into information; information turns into insights; insights turn into actionable plans; and actionable plans turn into measurable results. But the preceding does not happen by itself, just as data does not manage itself. It happens because of data leadership.

Anthony's greatest success in this book is to define the concept of data leadership. Success in creating value from data requires professionals with expertise in different disciplines. Data leadership is deciding which disciplines are needed, and to what degree, in order to obtain a business goal, and then coordinating the professionals and their work to create the engine for data-driven business improvement. Often what you do *not* do is as important as what you *do* do. Data leadership is making those decisions. The outcome of data leadership is trust. Trust that the data expresses corporate truth. Trust that decisions made using that data will be sound. Trust that data leadership has converted the potential of value of data into actual realized value.

In the world of business transformation, "best practices" is a common phrase, but it is not an analytic framework. If you measure best practices by what your peers are doing, and they are not doing it well, then doing it as well as they are doing it is not a terribly useful "best" of anything. "Best of breed" is a better business goal. It is adopting the best ways of accomplishing something by looking across industries to find what is done best and how. If your company needs to improve cybersecurity, then look to companies such as financial institutions that have devoted the time, resources, and technology to develop and implement the leading level of protection.

Evaluating this book in the context of these principles, we find: it is not too long and not too short, it is not too theoretical and not too entangled in a morass of detail, and it does not focus on business leadership at the expense of data leadership. It is a best of breed book on how to turn the potential of data into actual value. It reflects the time Anthony has spent working with data, the resources he has marshaled to make data an effective change agent in the various roles in which he has served, and his knowledge of how to use technology in combination with data. Put concisely, the value of the book is Anthony's skill is showing us what success looks like and how to get there.

William A. Tanenbaum
Mr. Tanenbaum is the leader of the AI & Data Practice
Group of the law firm of Moses & Singer LLP.

INTRODUCTION

DATA, WE'RE NOT MAD, JUST DISAPPOINTED

Data is lazy. It sits in files or databases, minding its own business but not accomplishing very much. Data is like someone in their midtwenties, living with their parents, who won't get off the couch and make something of their life.

Data is also the closest thing to truth we have in our organizations.

Data informs us about our businesses, and then we can either use that knowledge to improve what we do or decide that change is hard and go back to punching the clock, blindly hoping what we've always done will keep working. It is up to us—business professionals, executives, managers, frontline workers, entrepreneurs, all with the ability to be data leaders, regardless of whether the main functions of our jobs are related specifically to data—to motivate data to get up off the proverbial couch and make our organizations more successful!

In business, this means using data to understand

organizational processes and opportunities and then doing things better to improve our business outcomes. Sounds straightforward, right?

The problem is we are generally awful at turning the potential of data into something of actual value.

At one extreme, we have the most innovative companies doing unbelievable things with data and analytics, like when SpaceX successfully launched a rocket into space and then used real-time analytics to control and safely land an unmanned booster rocket upright on a barge floating in the ocean. Seeing a video of the rocket landing backward for the first time, the most rational response a person can have is to say, "These special effects look totally fake."

But they aren't special effects at all. They're real life!* And now, rockets are landing backward all over the place like it's no big deal. Cars are logging millions of autonomous miles, we talk to our TVs, and everybody carries a device in their pocket that can instantly connect them to the answer to nearly any question they can imagine. And that last one has been the case for over a decade!

All these things are amazing, every single day. It is an incredible time to be alive, and we should all be walking around astonished by what surrounds us and in awe of what awaits us beyond the horizon.

Instead, our expectations have risen with these technological capabilities, and we tend to have diminished tolerance for failures to meet these higher standards. If Netflix buffers for

---

* Unless, of course, it turns out we really are living in a simulation like the Matrix or something.

five seconds on our sixty-five-inch TV, we call it a piece of junk. If we request a password reset email and it doesn't immediately hit our inbox, we assume the company has been hacked and we start making plans to cancel our account and move to a competitor.

In our personal lives, we have such constantly profound data-driven experiences that it is especially frustrating in our work lives when we can't even get the numbers on two reports to match! How is it that we can go from literally talking to our entertainment devices at home to feeling like we are back in the dark ages of the 1990s when we head to work?

It used to be that we went to work to access the good stuff. Just twenty years ago, the technology capabilities at the office were far superior to those that individuals could own, mostly because the costs of high technology were out of the reach of individual consumers. Only businesses with big checkbooks could afford the big servers and the software applications to run on them.

Sure, businesses today still have the big checkbooks and an ability to buy fancy technologies far beyond our consumer-grade phones. And clearly some, like the backward-rocket-landing ones, are putting that technology to productive use. But then why do so many of our companies have such difficulty with something as simple as basic reporting?

It's because this is not a technology issue at all. It's about how we're using (or failing to use) that technology to leverage the information it gives us. Though data analytics almost always *involves* technology, it is not fundamentally *about* technology. Data is the result of our best attempts to record truths related to our businesses. Data analytics then evaluates and applies these truths to influence business activities so that future truths will, hopefully, improve by comparison.

Sometimes I wonder if organizations are even serious about being competitive within their industries. We see incredible innovation happening around us, but most of our organizations have failed to fully capitalize on the power contained in our data. We create pretty visualizations to obscure the unreliability of our data, and when we do luck into real data-driven insights, we often ignore them and revert to making decisions based on emotion or gut instinct.

Data is quickly becoming our most abundant resource while simultaneously propelling us to new heights in our ability to squander valuable things.

Our organizations currently find themselves largely incapable of harnessing the riches that data can provide. Instead, we find ourselves at greater risk, fearing data breaches and privacy violations that make the evening news and the trending topics on Twitter. It is not that we think data is worthless. Far from it!

Data being valuable is the premise on which I've spent decades building my career. The executives I encounter across every industry now see the potential value in data but struggle knowing what to do about it. Developing data-centric technology systems, growing consulting organizations, and leading massive change initiatives from the trenches have taught me how to navigate the innumerable complexities amid turning data into business success. Data leadership is a topic that connects everything I've learned, and the lessons in this book represent my life's work and my best attempt to save you from many years of trial and error, plenty of questionable career decisions, and at least one overpriced piece of sports memorabilia.

Data is complex, just like the truths it attempts to describe. There are different perspectives, and it may not always be easy to identify which of those perspectives are correct in which circumstances. The systems and processes to record and relay data must serve many different purposes and have significant technology and business considerations and implications. Though the complexity is palpable (especially at large scale), if we can break it down into smaller, more actionable chunks, we will find data excellence is within our reach.

Beyond the pure joy that comes from turning bits of information into real impact, in the next few years, any organization that does not become fundamentally data driven will inevitably be destroyed by their competition, whether current adversaries or new disruptors.

I once had an employer tell me I couldn't put a statement like that into a white paper because it was too provocative. I countered with, "But it is true, and it is also incredibly important. Shouldn't we share this with people?"

Long story short, I don't work there anymore.

....

Never be afraid to speak the truth just because someone might be uncomfortable with the consequences.

....

The idea that some organizations (and even entire industries) are still afraid to acknowledge that data competency is a requirement of competitiveness makes me chuckle and/or want to cry, depending on the day. Becoming proficient at turning data into improved business outcomes is now required for any organization to thrive. The competitive advantages gained by establishing a deep and detailed understanding of today's truths will uncover countless opportunities otherwise hidden from our view. If we do not, our competitors will, and they are probably already ahead in the journey.

What is scarier than the fact that data excellence is now necessary (not just helpful) for success is that the bar of reasonable competence is moving so high, so fast, that I fear many of our existing organizations will simply disappear rather than adapt quickly and remain competitive.

If this all seems a little strange or esoteric, don't worry. This whole introduction is like a data-flavored amuse-bouche (and if you needed to look that up, that makes two of us!). Throughout this book, we will cover so much about data and leadership and how together they drive organizational success, it will become second nature by the time you are done reading (or listening, if you've chosen the audiobook option with its lush baritone vocals).

And I guess now is as good a time as any to address my writing style. Some may call it "informal" whereas others, like my seventh-grade teacher (Mrs. Nelson), would probably say the style is "linguistically a poor choice for the topic of discussion." I like to think of it as a little more approachable than your typical data or business book, but mostly I needed to keep us both awake while exploring subjects that can be a bit on the dry side. This does not mean I'm any less (or more) qualified, knowledgeable, or passionate about data leadership than if I wrote the way my public school education taught me. It's just that I'm trying to make seventy-odd thousand words of data management and organizational theory a little more tolerable for all of us.

By studying the lessons in this book, you will learn how to maximize the value of data. You will see how it all fits together and will change the future of your organization. Whether you are an executive, sales rep, department head, copy editor, data scientist, or database administrator, this book is for you. It does not matter your role, just that you think data might help in some way.

If nothing else, remember that here we are among friends and that if we fail to deliver on the potential of our data, our companies are doomed. No pressure!

Let's get started.

PART 1

DATA LEADERSHIP FOUNDATIONS

1

THE VALUE OF DATA LEADERSHIP

WHAT MAKES DATA SO VALUABLE ANYWAY?

People generally acknowledge that data is valuable. If you walked into a random business somewhere and asked them if their data is valuable, you would get a bunch of nodding heads who were probably just being polite before they call security. But if, to avoid alarming everyone, you scheduled a proper meeting or focus group and asked the same question, they would almost certainly agree their business data is valuable. After all, hackers break the law to access organizations' data all the time, so it must be worth something, right?

Before we go further, let's just assume everybody is right: data is valuable. The more interesting question is "Why is data valuable?"

You can use data in a report, maybe run some metrics, inform an insight or two. But what makes those actions valuable? And not just *theoretically* valuable but *actually* valuable? Like real dollars, pounds, and euros valuable?

It's not as immediately obvious as something data related should be, is it?

That's because we get so lost in doing "data stuff" that we've lost sight of what even makes data valuable in the first place! We pull data, we nod our heads, we talk and talk and talk, and in the end, we have no earthly idea why we're doing any of this. It's time to wake up!

Everything we talk about in this book centers on using data to create something of value. Let's refer to this as *data value*.

Think of data value as the ultimate measure of the true benefits our data sprockets and widgets give to our customers. This depends on not just what we provide to them but how well our consumers use our outputs (their inputs) to turn the potential value into real outcomes.

....

Data value is the difference in business outcomes *with* data versus what could be achieved *without* data.

....

Realize that data value is not really about *data* at all. It is about the positive change in business outcomes that happens by using data. And just as important is understanding the inverse relationship: if our actions related to gathering, interpreting, and using data create no positive differential in business outcomes, then we have done nothing of value.

In more practical terms, if we deliver a report that fails to change anybody's behavior and thus creates no change in business outcome, then how could the real resources we used in creating that report be justified?

But data value can also be more nuanced. In my home suburb near Chicago, they tore down the long-shuttered Kmart to make way for a Mariano's grocery store. The Dominick's grocery a half mile down the street had shut down a couple of years earlier after succumbing to competitive pressures chain wide. It now sits empty. The former location of the Dominick's was admittedly a bit awkward to access, but why go through the effort of a teardown/rebuild of an old Kmart when another, better-equipped facility was empty nearby?

Data value! Mariano's recognized that while location is important, there was an opportunity to build an entirely new facility with plenty of parking and all the other amenities their customers value. They determined this would help their store stand out among crowded but aging grocery store competition in the local area. And in the years since they opened, Mariano's has been the go-to premium grocery store option for miles around!

The implications of this outcome are significant: one fast-growing grocery store brand replaced a dying one a half mile away and was built on a property that used to house a failed precursor to Walmart and Amazon. A grocery store! This is a classic case study of old-school, low-margin businesses being disrupted by newcomers willing to take chances based on data.

WE CAN'T MANAGE WHAT WE DON'T MEASURE

If we think data-driven strategy and operational efficiencies are not being leveraged by the upstarts in our own industries, then we are missing everything. If we want our organizations to remain relevant, we must maximize the use of data to get better at what we do best. And this starts with really understanding how data value is quantified.

....

Data value is measured in three ways:
- Revenue
- Cost
- Risk

These are the *only* ways data value is created.

....

Our efforts will have costs, which is a decline in value, and we hope the decline is more than offset by a combination of positive impacts. Increasing revenue and decreasing costs are straightforward: money in and money out. It is helpful to consider risk separately because risk management effectiveness cannot be measured by looking directly at results; the sample size of events that happen is too small to gauge the optimal strategy. It's like insurance.

Also note that dollars and other hard currencies may not be the only unit of measure, since the objectives of an organization may be to provide another outcome, such as a public service or charitable function. If we think of "increasing revenue" as the organization's ability to deliver more of that service or function, "decreasing costs" as improving the operating efficiency of delivery, and "managing risk" as managing risk, then we are all set! We may need to do a little semantic translation of some of the concepts, but the concept of data value very much applies in any type of organization.

The opportunity to deliver on the promise of data to our organizations is beckoning. Consider recent history and where it's all heading from here. Looking back at workplace pictures from the 1990s, you might think, "That's so cute!" Things were so much simpler then, with our enormous computers and phones with cords. We had predictions about what the future would hold but overemphasized physical innovations like flying cars over the impact of the internet and supercomputers in every pocket. We are now in the middle of a big societal shift, with a front-row seat to watch history repeat itself!

Today we are far beyond where we were, but nowhere near where we are going. That is, we are part of the way through a long journey!

Tremendous changes are happening with data and technology. We are transforming from batch processing to continuous availability and reliance on constant uptime. We once had to go sit at a desk to amplify our human capabilities with computers, then one day, laptops let us work from the couch, and eventually mobile devices allowed instant access wherever we want it. Evolving rapidly now, the Internet of Things (internet-connected devices with sensors, cameras, and interactive features) has created a world where we are living with an array of connected devices that are always on, always monitoring, and hopefully always improving our lives. Shh! Amazon Alexa probably heard that, and we don't want to make her mad.

Everything is trending smaller, faster, and more connected, to the point that physical hardware endpoints are often reduced to their purely physical role. From RFID chips to beacons to fitness watches—by offloading the complex data processing, networks of cheap, independent sensors can become ubiquitous.

The stakes couldn't be higher than they are with data. Why have we not fixed this by now? It's not like data wasn't around twenty or thirty years ago. It almost feels like we are honoring some silly tradition mandating that we stink at data management, but the pain is getting far worse because the pace of data growth, along with the technology capabilities that supercharge it, are increasing exponentially in their power. The gap between the exceptional data-driven organizations and the marginal ones is also ever increasing, and we are seeing the consequences everywhere we look, even with our hometown grocery stores.

We pay so much attention to data and technology that we may be inclined to think that data and technology are where we will find the solution to our challenges with creating data value. I believe this is wrong. The answers to realizing the value of data are found within the people and organizational dynamics of our companies. This book explains why this is the case and helps us understand what we need to do to overcome these challenges and create the data-driven organizations that will succeed in the coming years.

Data value is the common thread, and it is up to those of us who see its potential to take action to make it real. After all, the folks who do not yet see the value in data will not be the ones to pave the way.

DATA LEADERSHIP MAXIMIZES DATA VALUE

As was mentioned in the introduction, data doesn't do anything by itself. When we say *data* in the context of data value and data leadership, we also mean all the technology capabilities, interfaces, artifacts, insights, actions, etc., that are related to the data. But make no mistake, data is the star of this show! Data is the influencer of value-creating actions, and the role of data leadership is to give data's direction maximum reach.

There is an old-school discipline related to optimizing data efforts called "data management." This is a collection of data-related functions that people conduct to ostensibly make data better. These are things like metadata management, data quality, and data governance, all of which you will find covered in detail later as part of the data leadership framework. We didn't invent these concepts with data leadership, but we're evolving the *why* and *how* we choose to invest our efforts at any point in time.

Data leadership gives us the ability to turn what feels like an impossible challenge into an engine of data-driven business improvement. The magic of data leadership is in balancing the various aspects of data, focusing our limited energy to create the most data value overall.

Maximizing data value is the most important thing.

We need to stop pretending that there is intrinsic value in investing energies in data capabilities and instead focus on creating value within our businesses as our top priority, with data as our guide. Traditional data management approaches do not focus enough on the contribution to real business outcomes, and this leads to wasted efforts and less impactful data in the end.

Businesses typically choose their investments based on

an expected return. This comes from increases to revenues, decreases to costs, or improvements in risk management. These measurements sound familiar, right? The sad truth is most data management efforts do not even know their intended return on investment (ROI), let alone the returns they achieve. This is no way to run a business, and it is no way to lead data-driven change efforts. Data leadership keeps us later focused on the most important thing, maximizing data value.

Data leadership is how we choose to apply our limited resources to maximizing data value.

There are so many options for how our time, money, and other resources may be applied, and breaking them down and understanding when and how to apply them is the focus of much of this book. We will explore some of the foundational disciplines of data management and some of the technologies that can help us amplify them. These are the collection of tools in our tool belt, so it is imperative that we know *what* they are and *how* they impact data value. But just as important, we must learn *when* and *why* we should put these tools to work, since our resources are limited and we want to maximize the benefits we get from them.

Consider data leadership the factory where we build the data sprockets and widgets that our customers will use. We may create data capabilities with a lot of potential value, but until these data capabilities are applied, the value in them is unrealized.

This is a point worth repeating:

- *Potential value* is what it is possible to accomplish.
- *Realized value* is what was accomplished.

Which of those is more, um, *valuable*? Yeah, realized value. Because of this, data value is defined by realized value, not by data's potential value. And by extension, it is why data leadership is so much more valuable than traditional data management.

By connecting data efforts directly to business outcomes, data leadership builds business successes directly from the data we think is valuable.

Data value is the barometer by which we should judge our data leadership performance, and it extends to everyone and everything working with information in our businesses, regardless of whether they identify as data leaders. It is not enough to have information. It is not even enough to use the information to do something. The information must drive a result with consequences (hopefully positive ones!). Like anything we do with data, maximizing our outcomes begins with measuring.

Priorities within each organization will vary, as will the appropriate balance of what will be needed to maximize data value, but that's why we are data leaders! If creating data value were as simple in practice as in concept, we'd just be data middle-of-the-packers. Because we're setting a high bar, let's make sure we understand the data value concept completely.

First, consider a simple example. Sales data for a restaurant is correlated with weather conditions using a simple regression model. Tomorrow's forecast is for unseasonably cool temperatures, so the owner decides that they will need one fewer lobster in the tank. A few dollars are saved, and Pinchy lives to fight another day. So in this simple (but heartfelt) example, costs are decreased directly due to data analysis.

Now for a more complicated scenario. Company B has decided to sponsor a project that will, among other things, perform a data lineage analysis for a set of core executive reports. The executive team uses these reports already but has identified inconsistencies in some of the numbers, and this has led to a general sense of distrust in the organization's data.

What will the value be of performing this data lineage analysis? Could be a lot of things, right? Perhaps once the executives regain their trust in the data, they will be able to make decisions more quickly, exploiting new business opportunities (and increasing revenue). Or once the differences in numbers are better understood, they will reduce the effort spent manually reconciling everything (and decreasing costs). The managing risks possibility is obvious as well—compromised or inaccurate data could lead to many bad business outcomes.

Here's the thing: it's not enough to simply identify where data value might come from. It is imperative to take a baseline measurement of the current situation and then measure again and compare once the project is complete. It may not be possible to get a fully quantitative measurement, but even a ballpark/ order-of-magnitude assessment is better than relying on people's selective memory the next time we want to propose a data value–enhancing project within our organization.

In our report example, we could directly measure the amount of time being spent on report creation, plus how much time it takes to reconcile the nonmatching numbers. We could survey the executives to determine their current level of trust in the data and how willing they are to use data to drive their decisions and activities, and that will help us link to the data's measurable difference in business outcomes. Even if the measurements are subjective, we can at least quantify our impacts down the road once additional efforts are underway.

The pattern highlighted by the preceding examples shows these three data value measurements are often hiding in plain sight. They are usually there, but many times we either do not know to or choose to take the time to track them.

If we fail to benchmark at the outset of a project, we lose an opportunity to measure data value. Worse, we lose the ability to make our own efforts as efficient and impactful as possible.

By always pushing to understand the real data value, we will hopefully avoid the activities that feel like productive work but fail to produce tangible results.

WHAT ABOUT DATA GOVERNANCE? ISN'T THAT A THING?

Data governance is a common endeavor for organizations that want to do more with data. This is the traditional way we create structure around the data assets of an organization, including establishing standards, policies, and guidelines for use. Data governance also provides a mechanism where decisions around data can be made and where conflicts can be resolved. It is one of the best ways to invest a lot of resources but realize very little from the efforts.

For example, if we set up a data governance organization, we are committing to a lot of effort with several degrees of separation between the data governance activities and the three ways data value is created. People will meet, talk a lot about data, and come away with decisions and artifacts but little that translates directly to business outcomes. This likely creates a lot of potential value, but the realized value of data governance is notoriously difficult to quantify because it is so far removed from the core business outcomes of revenue, costs, and risk.

Before we start to question why anybody tries to do data governance at all, which isn't a totally unfair question, we should understand that creating potential value is still important. We devote a significant part of this book to the ways we create potential data value. But even if we have all the potential in the world, not unlike the next overhyped sports star, if we can't put points on the board, our potential will be quickly forgotten. If data is not driving meaningful, measurable changes in business outcomes, then the data provides no value. It is really that simple.

One of the great ironies of data professionals is we often fail to measure our own performance the way we advocate everybody else does. This may be due to the several degrees of separation that exist between data value–driven projects and increasing revenue, decreasing costs, and managing risks. We do things, and then somebody else does something, then one more person does something, and *then* data value is realized, maybe, but we're not entirely sure. And after all this, we wonder why data governance projects struggle? Too often they do not even bother trying to justify their existence!

Due to the number of leaps between the investments and the returns, data-related initiatives will not succeed without overwhelmingly clear business impacts.

It is unfortunate that there are so many steps between our data efforts and tangible business value, but that's how it is. This is also why data management is commonly misunderstood, and those of us dedicating our careers to it are having such incredible adventures transforming our organizations! That sounded a bit sarcastic, but it's true.

There are simpler paths to personal career success. There are more financially lucrative ones. However, there are no roles more central to the success of organizations across all industries than that of the data leader. Our titles and specific responsibilities will vary, but our commitment to creating data value will prove to be one of the most influential differentiators of tomorrow's businesses.

The rest of this book will help you build the perspective and skills to create data value, and we will refer to this chapter's concepts frequently. Consider this book your sharpening stone to realign your focus on what matters when the real world proves distracting. Here we will talk about how things *should* be and what you *should* do in response. In practice, it is never so clear, and every decision comes with a trade-off. We all have day jobs and responsibilities, never enough time or resources, office politics, people who don't get it, people who don't care, and if we're lucky, personal lives we like to enjoy occasionally.

So let's take a breath, maybe softly whisper "data value" to ourselves a couple of times, and then turn the page—both literally and figuratively. It is not trivial to be at the center of our organization's future success, and many of us may not have intended to be here.

2

WHAT WE SHOULD
DO DIFFERENTLY

THERE IS NO SHORTAGE OF IMPROVEMENT OPPORTUNITIES

Data value makes good sense. It is logical, measurable, and a concept that we can drive a whole bunch of meaningful activities from. That's lucky for us, because many of our organizations are currently operating as if they have no clue why they are doing many of the data-related activities that consume so much time, energy, and financial resources.

This current lack of understanding of data value is evident through the interactions of our business and technology personnel. Technology organizations are where builders (programmers, database developers, networking, infrastructure, etc.) leverage their skills and experience to deliver solutions to help business-people do what they do faster, cheaper, and/or better. While it presumably started as a true partnership, over the years, the dynamic between business and technology folks has become more unidirectional, with the business articulating needs and the technology people filling the orders as best they can.

Communications between these two groups are often ineffi-cient at best and commonly completely dysfunctional. The process looks something like this:

- A businessperson will ask a technology person for something like a report or new data-centric application. Most technology initiatives with funding start with the business having an idea of something they want.
- There will be some back-and-forth ironing out all the business requirements to ensure there is enough detail to drive a technical specification.
- To gain better understanding of what the businessperson is looking for, the technology persons will at some point ask questions like "How will you use this?," "What will you use this for?," "How will this help you?," "What do you need from this?," and "What are your business requirements?"
- The businessperson responds with some amount of detail, and often there are a couple of rounds of revisions. At some point, the team feels that the design is complete, and then the technology people go into their caves, emerging sometime later with a solution that checks all the boxes.

In an "agile" shop, the tech team may emerge more frequently with smaller improvements to workshop, but that doesn't really matter here. The fact is that they already botched the design, so however they want to build the wrong thing doesn't change the fact that they are, in fact, building the wrong thing.

Based on our definition of data value, did you catch where in this typical process the IT team lost their way?

It was when IT asked the business what they want. Asking those "What do you want?" type of questions comes from a one-sided perspective and leads to an inability to gauge value, drive priorities, or have a meaningful two-way collaboration about the design of what is being built.

WRONG:

- What will you use this for?
- How will this help you?
- What do you need from this?
- What are your requirements?

INSTEAD ASK:

- When we give you this, what will you do differently?
- How will this new process or report help you increase revenue, decrease costs, or mitigate risks?
- What would you do instead if you did not have this?

What defines the wrong questions is that they are *incomplete*. They are only looking at part of the equation, and because of this, they are ineffective at helping us understand what we should do to create the most data value.

....

When our design questions look only at the end state, we can't maximize a change in business outcomes because we don't know the starting point.

....

Nothing better reflects this disconnect than "business requirements." As a term and as a philosophy, business requirements should be banished to the recycling bin of history. We could not choose a more unidirectional, condescending, yet sadly accurate label to illustrate the current state of business-technology interactions. The concept of business requirements is completely opposed to everything we should stand for as data leaders.

Please allow me to explain.

The way it typically works is business requirements are mapped in detail by a business analyst, which leads to a technical design that accommodates those requirements and to the people who build it all. Some of these tasks can be performed by the same people in roles that cross over, but there are usually multiple people involved as it progresses. Regardless of precisely how many people or steps are involved, outcomes suffer when the flow of information is too unidirectional.

Think of a restaurant. The hungry customer reads the menu, and based on a highly complex algorithm of what looks good (they had tuna yesterday, and beets are gross), they choose to have a salad with chicken. The server then communicates the order to the kitchen staff, who begin preparing the order. But they spill the last container of chicken on the floor right as they start to make the salad! If they have no ability to send this new, unfortunate information back to the customer, they might make an even more unfortunate substitution of tuna (or worse, beets!) to the eventual chagrin of everyone involved.

Without an ability or desire to incorporate new information into their directives, businesses are hurting themselves. Things go on in the technology kitchen that, for the most part, the business is happy and better off not worrying about. But data and technology projects are more complex than salads, and by promoting a system of business requirements and technical execution, business customers are setting themselves up for unacceptable substitutions or the IT equivalent of dirty chicken.

IGNORING DATA RUINS ALL HOPE FOR MAXIMIZING DATA VALUE

How many technology systems have been adversely impacted because the business never gave IT a voice in design? Countless. I can promise you with 95 percent likelihood that in your organization, there is more than one technologist who has given up trying to do their best work because any time they suggest an alternative to a business requirement–driven design element, they are told to just get it done as originally specified.

As we defined earlier, data value comes from the difference in business outcomes. The only way to gauge that difference is to measure (or estimate) the starting and ending outcomes. Any project that relies only on vague directional guidance like "It will improve our customer service" or "The current system is too slow" is going to have suboptimal outcomes.

We should not ask, "What do you want?" or the equivalent. We should instead ask, "How can we create a solution that maximizes the improvement in business outcomes compared with the costs of developing that solution?" Granted, that may be a bit of a mouthful for one question, but the goal is to ask a series of questions to fully understand the following:

- **What is the starting point? What would the situation be if we do nothing? What are the likely business outcomes in the continuing status quo situation?**
- **How does the business envision its outcomes improving with this effort? Are there specific business outcome goals in mind? Who is responsible for these outcomes? Is that individual sponsoring this project effort? How will we measure the results for both the resources consumed and the impacts to revenues, costs, and risk management?**
- **How do the known costs align with available resources, given the current design? What is not yet known that the success of this project may depend on?**

Now we are directly addressing the value of data! We are having a conversation to predict the expected impact to revenue, cost, and risk mitigation. If we ask about a differential in outcome, we will establish a current baseline and a clear target result for the endeavor. Any specific design elements are calibrated against data value, and that leads us down a path to getting the benefits maximized compared to the costs of making it happen.

Perhaps more importantly, it begins to change the dynamics of the relationship between the business (requestor) and technology (requestee) from a unidirectional flow to a two-way collaboration. When we talk about maximizing the ultimate outcomes for the business, we become a team—mutually committed to finding the right path to the greatest business impact.

Technology folks have a tremendous knowledge of what is possible, which directly complements the business's in-depth understanding of what would be useful.

This is a departure from how things work in many organizations. Technology (and data) folks like to focus on their functional responsibilities and often do not get deep enough into the business impacts of what they do. On the flip side, when businesspeople oversee providing requirements to build new systems, they often define what they want in terms of what they have, and this will limit their ability to create innovative solutions that make the most of the latest technology capabilities that the technology folks really, really want to use!

The partnership *should be* amazing! It is like peanut butter and jelly, or peanut butter and chocolate, or even peanut butter and celery! (I could go for some peanut butter, apparently.) But for some reason, the IT and business groups often have less-than-stellar working relationships, and isn't getting our teams working better together the most important thing?

No, maximizing data value is the most important thing! Have you not been paying attention so far? But to be fair, if we want to maximize data value, fixing how our business and technology people work together is something we need to address.

3

BRIDGING THE DIVIDE BETWEEN IT AND THE BUSINESS

THE MOST IMPORTANT CHALLENGE FACING TODAY'S BUSINESSES

Quick review: Data is important. Technology amplifies it, and the business connects it to outcomes that are measurable and valuable. Data value is the equation we use to determine the effectiveness of actions and processes, and data leadership is how we strategically make the best investments of our various limited resources to maximize data value. All these are important concepts, underlying the role data plays in our organizations. They are also admittedly a bit esoteric and theoretical, which means we now need to get pragmatic.

Data is the very essence of our businesses and is in the complete control of information technology professionals.

Just reading the last sentence makes you feel uneasy, doesn't it? We agree data is important, so if we want to be a bit dramatic and say "data is the very essence of our businesses," we can probably get away with that. The second part is the scary part, as we are not so comfortable turning over something so important to those IT people. Thing is, though, it was the information systems that captured and stored all the data in the first place.

Now, it isn't a huge stretch to suggest that the business and IT do not generally get along great. But why has that relationship gotten so dysfunctional? Don't we realize how much we need each other? Do we need to talk about peanut butter some more? We're not in high school choosing lunchroom tables. We're already all stuck at the company table, so we should find a way to make the most of it!

Data was always controlled by information technology systems and people. Everyone else has finally recognized how important data is, so now they are afraid of IT mucking it up!

I have strong opinions on this one. Note that the following is highly subjective, a bit sensationalized, but earnestly drawn from decades of experience observing this dynamic relationship from several roles. Spoiler alert: I don't pick sides, but I do think we all have a lot of room for improvement.

MY PERSPECTIVE ON THE PERSPECTIVE OF THE IT FOLKS

IT people, and I identify myself as one, often see themselves as superheroes. We take insane requests from the business and use our technical wizardry to do magical things that nobody appreciates but should rightfully strike everyone to their core with awe. We get judged in black and white, while everybody else around here never seems to have any clear performance metrics. Everybody wants everything done immediately, with no respect for our systems development life cycle, but whenever the smallest thing goes wrong, it's IT's fault.

It's like we are being singled out and treated differently from everybody else. Those business folks never appreciate the complexity and the fact that we always manage to get stuff done, even though we've never been given the budget to address the looming technical debt that keeps growing after years of inadequate support from the business!

MY PERSPECTIVE ON THE PERSPECTIVE OF THE BUSINESS FOLKS

Businesspeople, who I also identify with, are perpetually frustrated with IT folks. The IT people seem to only say no, and even items that should be simple fixes take weeks or months, if they get addressed at all.

IT people are always complaining about being under-resourced, but the business does not have the resources to keep dumping into the vortex of technology when our ROI on these investments is questionable at best. Lots of times, when things do get done, they have a bunch of stability or reliability issues, and what they deliver may not even resemble what we wanted in the first place!

The IT people are constantly doing "maintenance" and "patch fixes" that never seem to do anything other than cause outages. We have a business to run, and too often we are held hostage by IT!

End scene.

Like I disclaimed, my scenarios may have been a bit amplified, but we can all likely relate to at least some of it. This mutual animosity between IT and the business has built up over decades of poor communication and a genuine lack of empathy among the different areas of our organizations. Because the pattern is so consistent, these feelings naturally transfer across different companies, so even getting new personnel will do little to remedy these chronic issues.

So it's time to start over. Even though I believe everything we've covered in this chapter so far is true, we need to forget it. We can't start here if we want to transform our businesses into nimble, high-functioning, data-driven organizations. We need to fix things even further upstream. So let's address the question that everybody should have been asking from the start of this: is this how we should really break down our organizations?

....

IT is a part of the business, just like every other department.

....

It is ridiculous that we bisect our organizations into the IT department and literally everybody else in the company, called "the business." It kind of seems like we are singling out the technology folks and treating them differently from the rest of the folks. Maybe this is the reason IT people feel like they are being singled out and treated differently from the rest of the folks.

In defense of *the rest of the folks*, technology people tend to be a bit different and do not always respond well when the business does try to communicate better. The tech people do voodoo with their JSON and APIs and Python and other strangely titled things they go to conferences to learn about. For instance, Splunk *can't* be a real thing, can it?

Maybe if these people are kept locked in their windowless caves in the basement and we pay them decently, they won't run off and leave the business folks to try to deal with it all. They will keep doing their jobs and keep the lights on and the systems running, and the business will get a new report or self-service data visualization tool occasionally.

This attitude is not at all irrational. People are busy and focused on their own jobs, not necessarily on how to gain the most competitive advantage by leveraging the nerds who don't like to talk to people. This used to be okay, back when individual servers were the size of rooms and you didn't always have a supercomputer in your pocket. The demands of today's businesses require much more than you can do on your own, and those IT folks hold the keys to your future success.

CAN'T WE ALL JUST GET ALONG? UM, CLEARLY NOT

Remember data value? Try creating some of that without relying on IT in some way. Also, please note, while I recognize it is against my principles to continue to refer to these groups as "IT" and "the business," there is a lot of work to be done before we can say those divisions no longer exist. So to make things simpler throughout this book, I'll continue using them. Just know I don't like it, and hopefully in the next edition, I will be able to say "the business" and "the business," and then it will be super clear to everybody. Until then, begrudgingly, I'm going to keep talking about "IT" and "the business."

An organization has a few choices when considering how to address the conflict between IT and the business.

Ignore it and hope for the best. This is the current approach employed by many businesses. It isn't working so far, but maybe things will turn around once the technology improves. That's a silly thought, but it's not silly to consider doing nothing. In fact, this is something we must always consider whenever we are attempting to create data value, and repairing the relationship between IT and the business is certainly part of that!

The benefits of this approach are that we can use our efforts in a more targeted way elsewhere and that we aren't asking everybody to change how they work. The downsides are that we do not fix the underlying problem and that this dysfunction will act like a tax, hurting every other initiative involving both IT and the business. Rats! This plan was sounding so good two sentences ago.

Redefine the relationship. The term "cross-functional teams" comes to mind. If we want IT and the business to start acting like one business, maybe it makes sense to mash them together and make them do everything as a team. This way, they'll hopefully start to develop empathy for each other and teach each other some new skills while they are at it.

The strength of this approach is that it directly addresses the root cause of the divide between IT and the business—that they have little empathy for each other because they do not really understand what the other does. If done well, this will transform your organization by supercharging productivity and employee satisfaction and retention and will likely get us promoted. The downside of this approach is that it is supremely disruptive to people's status quo, and if the transition is not proactively managed, we will encounter decreased productivity, lower employee satisfaction, and higher attrition; there's also a fair chance that it will fail entirely and we will end up no better or worse than before. We'll also probably get fired.

Blow it up completely. Some organizations see that they shouldn't choose Door Number 1, and Door Number 2 seems too risky, so they have tried to find a better path. An industry has developed that allows our organizations to outsource any of our IT-related functions, and because the folks performing the services are external to our own companies, they know if they don't perform, our companies can more easily replace them than our internal resources.

Positives include that this approach typically comes with some cost savings, due to either an offshoring arrangement or simply the economies of scale that the vendor firm has by spreading their systems, personnel, and practices across multiple clients. Outsourcing IT responsibilities may give companies the ability to flex more effectively, aligning the size of project teams to fit the increased demand of building something and then ramping down when in more of a maintenance mode. Also, attracting the talent we'd like to have internally may simply not be feasible. Public sector organizations, for example, often have difficulty recruiting the full-time talent they need, so the next best option is to bring in contractor assistance to help get the job done.

The negative with this approach is that an outsourcing strategy can create operational or strategic disconnects between the business itself and the systems and data the business relies on to be a business. Think of it this way: if data represents the essence of an organization and we outsource the technical responsibilities related to it, are we in danger of effectively selling our souls?

What should we do? Well, it depends. The answer is going to look a little different for every organization, but most will probably have parts of each of the above strategies. Frankly, the specific approach matters far less than the intent of those involved. If you can align people's interests in such a way that they are committed to working together to make your company awesome, then use whatever interaction coordination mechanism you like.

Now that we understand the basics of the problem and the three main ways to address it, we find ourselves in need of some good, old-fashioned leadership. This can sometimes be accomplished purely by leaders outside the technology organization, but typically it is best to involve IT leadership in this kind of transformation. It may not be the *same* IT leadership that got us into the mess in the first place, but if we choose a path that involves people needing to change, we are going to need help wherever we can find it.

It's easy (and kinda fun) to blame all these challenges of IT solely on our technology personnel; after all, they need to be responsible for their own jobs. The chief information officers (CIOs) sit at the top of the technology pyramid, so they rightfully get the lion's share of the blame. We will not correct the broken dynamics between IT and the rest of the business unless our CIOs do a better job of contributing business relevance at the senior-most levels of our organizations. That is obviously necessary and should be the first thing we change.

Don't hold your breath.

Asking the average CIO to all of a sudden be a capable

business leader is like asking a fish to go for a jog around the lake. Most CIOs have spent twenty to thirty years working in technology; they are typically ill-equipped to do the jobs we are asking of them. Spending a career in this mess is not the way to change things, and remember, these breakdowns between IT and the business are not entirely IT's fault, so it's just not reasonable to expect our CIOs to magically have it all figured out despite being in the middle of it all for their entire careers.

When I teach basic management training, the first tenet I explain to students is that for each one of your employees, you must balance the empowerment you give them with the accountability you are asking of them. In other words, you must put people in a position to be successful—the more you need from them, the more control you must cede to them.

We cannot ethically hold someone accountable for something we never gave them the opportunity to do.

If you want to see the most egregious examples of this, go find a CISO (chief information security officer). Few can implement the controls they think are essential, but all are first under the bus the moment a breach happens. It's like the CISO is just a bull's-eye for buses. Just go stand over here in this special CISO lane, and the bus will be along at some point! Thank you for your service!

Take the CISO, move a step higher up the food chain, and you have the situation many CIOs find themselves in. They sit at the top of often-large departments where their primary responsibility is frequently to be the top technology order taker and scapegoat.

For those of us who haven't had this kind of role in an organization, this description may seem extreme. Let's consider this: who does the CFO call if her laptop is slow, or who does an executive vice president call when her Outlook keeps crashing on startup? Some will dutifully delegate to their assistants or call the help desk themselves, but when it's important they get a solution fast, the CIO gets that call directly, every time.

As much as we'd like to change things starting with the CIO, it's going to take more than that. Today's challenges are the result of decades of poor engagement between the business and IT, and to change it, we are going to have to teach our CIOs to become business leaders. This will only happen if they are given an opportunity to learn and partner with the business (empowerment) as they deliver the data value necessary to empower business outcomes (accountability).

WE ARE ALL "THE BUSINESS." YES, EVEN IT

It's clear that things aren't working between IT and everybody else. If we realign to embrace our shared responsibility of maximizing data value and focus on how we can maximize business outcomes together, then we'll start to improve this dysfunctional relationship. Preaching data value won't be enough. After all, how many business or technology people are really committed to overcoming systemic ineffectiveness in communication between diverse sets of stakeholders?

I'm not sure most people would be committed enough to carefully read that last sentence, let alone do something about it. We should probably just give up and deal with the fact that business and IT folks are incompatible and we're all doomed.

Of course not! We're going to fix this! But we've got to break it down before we build it back up, so now seems as good a time as any to hit rock bottom. It is about one crucially important fact that we must keep in mind if we want people to do something that helps us: people care about themselves more than they will ever care about you.

....

The number one lesson of human motivation is that nobody cares about you as much as you do.

....

Your needs, your great ideas, your kids, your important projects, your future, your vacation, your blah-blah-blah. When we talk, most of the time people are filtering every single one of our words through their "how does this impact me" lens. They will smile and nod all day until something we are saying hits close enough to home. People, seemingly out of some evolutionary necessity, only care about adding benefits, lessening pain, or managing risk on their own personal level.

That is unless we are talking about truly charitable acts done for the benefit of humanity by people who have a strong personal motivation to make these contributions—*and it's a trap!* Seemingly charitable acts are still personally motivated by people who want to feel good about themselves and their contributions; these are just not *monetarily* motivated self-interests. Did we just inadvertently disparage charitable acts? Not at all, but we did acknowledge that even helping others traces its underlying motivations to serving ourselves, at least in part.

It's okay though. Don't give up yet! Self-interested motivations give us something to work with because we can reasonably expect that if we can appeal to selfish individuals (i.e., all of us), then we can effect change. If we can achieve positive net impacts, regardless of the motivations, then we will be able to achieve data value creation. And isn't that the most important thing?

Yes. That time, it wasn't a trick. Good job!

....

Balance empowerment and accountability, and then motivate through aligned incentives. Sounds easy. It isn't.

....

When incentives are aligned to the motivations of those whose behavior we want to influence, requests are aligned with empowerment, and the net benefits outweigh the net pain, people will accomplish amazing things.

Data leadership is fundamentally rooted in this truth, and we will spend a lot of time in the remaining chapters discussing techniques to achieve it. We must always remember that people are watching out for number one more than anything else, and if we are going to ask them to do something, there had better be something in it for them too! This could be as little as pizza or as much as a partnership. Or a jet. I can only imagine how motivating a jet would be, though that ROI would need to be something spectacular!

Sadly, however, benefiting the organization's profitability

rarely provides enough motivation to get people to do more than attend a meeting or two. We will have to be more creative if we want data-driven initiatives to take flight. We'll get into this more later, but even expecting people to act in their own best interests is an oversimplification. People will more easily act when motivated by fun or convenience, and yes, they will even on occasion act out of wanting to help somebody. Selfishly wanting to help somebody usually, but hey, we'll take what we can get!

Earlier we talked about balancing empowerment with accountability within our teams. The same holds true as we work with areas outside our direct organizational lines. If you happen to be or aspire to be a chief data officer, you will find that as your profile rises, so does the percentage of time you spend trying to manage or influence initiatives that span far beyond your direct teams.

One of the most prevalent and failure ridden of these endeavors is that of data governance. Most organizations attempting data governance today are on their third or fourth ride on this merry-go-round. Sadly, most still have no chance of succeeding. In the upcoming chapter, we talk about how to rethink this whole data governance thing that so many of us get worked up about.

4

THE TRUTH ABOUT TRADITIONAL DATA GOVERNANCE

DATA GOVERNANCE FOR DATA LEADERSHIP

We have been talking about the breakdowns between the business and technology folks in an organization, and we identified the challenges around incentives and motivating people. These all become big factors as we try to keep data governance's momentum going, but they are not why most data governance is flawed out of the gate.

Since some of us may not know much about data governance beyond the references in this book, let's start with a definition. This is probably a good idea for everybody here, in fact, because it seems like this data management space has a wide variety of definitions. Here's one that complements data leadership well:

....

Data governance is how we coordinate people to help our organizations get the most from our data.

....

Data governance typically leads us to clarify definitions, provide data lineage maps, and generally try to make things more transparent so people *can work with data more efficiently.* We might even see a parallel between what data leadership is doing for the business and what data governance is doing for the data itself. They both seek to deliberately improve things people would do otherwise.

Data governance should help people spend less time asking questions *about* data and more time answering questions *with* data.

I think the definition above is what we should be aiming for with data governance, yet when we observe data governance in the wild, it seems that many organizations' working definition of data governance is "Have sparsely attended meetings to create data rules that nobody else knows or cares about and to complain that people do not understand or appreciate what we are trying to do with data governance."

And based on our definition, did we just do some data governance ourselves by clarifying definitions? You betcha. We didn't even need twelve people in a meeting to talk about it! That crack on pointless meetings may feel a little harsh, but in reality, the most common pattern of data governance attempts in organizations looks something like this:

- **Executive sponsor gets excited about data, decides to do data governance (again) but get it right this time.**

- Go-getters (aspiring data leaders) do a bunch of hard work to get things moving.
- The data governance program is launched with great fanfare.
- Data governance council meets, often monthly, starting with near-universal participation with the exception of an executive or two who doesn't really understand why they are there.
- At each meeting, data is talked about, next steps are defined, and people are assigned tasks.
- Between meetings, sometimes people do what they were assigned, but often they "didn't have time," but *this month* they will absolutely get to it.
- Over time, meeting attendance diminishes and/or the meeting frequency slows down because there is not enough for the council to do.
- After twelve to twenty-four months, the whole thing sort of fades away, and nobody seems to notice.

Many data governance programs end up as pointless, half-complete, miserable uses of people's time and energy. If we identify the purpose of most data governance endeavors, it comes down to some mash-up like "making data a more transparent, usable asset that helps facilitate business operations and ensure compliance with regulatory mandates."

Is that a helpful undertaking? Of course.

Will it ever work? Nope. Why in the world would we focus on data governance this way?

Sadly, this general pattern happens more than it doesn't. What's the problem here? Why doesn't this top-down data governance model seem to work?

....

Getting a bunch of folks together in a room to talk about data creates no data value by itself.

....

Putting together policies, establishing data owners, documenting data definitions—none of these things directly creates data value. And frankly, they are so many steps removed from actual data value creation that most data governance organizations have no idea how much net positive impact their efforts have on the business. C'mon! We need to be better than that.

Will it be important to have some meetings to talk about data? Probably. But we need more direction and more concrete outcomes. We need accountability to balance the empowerment, and we'd better find a way to impact the business quickly.

Data governance should remove friction from everything we do with data. If we can quickly and clearly reference the definition of a data element, that can save us a lot of time and energy, helping us continue on our path unabated. But what if we aren't yet moving? A frictionless environment doesn't do us a lot of good.

In fact, data governance in the absence of other momentum is like an '83 Ford Mustang convertible with bald tires in the middle of an icy parking lot in February—it's not helping us get anywhere. But in a few months when the weather is nice, we will be so glad we have it because it will be so useful then, and that's exactly when the motor gives out completely and we have to go back to riding our bicycles!

We don't need data governance. We *need* to create data value. Data governance is part of how we do that.

Doing data governance to address some future pain or to help solve some ambiguous future efficiency goal is simply a subtle way to avoid accountability. Instead, find a way to add data value now.

Chances are to do this, data governance will be involved in some way, so let's build it over time in alignment with the actual value it contributes. But what if we don't have the option to take a ninja-like approach to building data governance? What if we have been told that data governance is what we need to do as our job? What if we are doing lots of things with data, we have plenty of momentum, and data governance is really what we need to remove friction so that we can work better with data?

That's great! We certainly want to do data governance if it is well justified, but it is important for people to realize that we should be deliberate in our objectives with data governance. It is not an end unto itself but must be used judiciously as a means to an end. In fact, within the data leadership framework that we will cover soon, data governance is not even designated as a separate discipline. This is because data governance is everywhere data is, involved with everything we do with data, both organizationally and individually.

Bob Seiner, famous for his book *Non-Invasive Data Governance*, starts many of his talks by asking the audience who in the room has data governance in their organization. Around half the room will raise their hands. Then Bob tells everyone to raise their hands because every organization is governing data somehow. It just may not be well organized, coordinated, or effective. His point is that some set of norms and expectations, even if not proactively managed, still influences folks' data-related behaviors, and we will accomplish far more with our data if we put some structures in place so those norms and expectations are more consistent and reliable.

I agree with Bob as well as the other data governance experts out there, and I believe data leadership complements their work— the other side of the same coin, if you will. While data governance provides guidance, it does not inherently build momentum, which is *exactly* what data leadership is designed to do.

> **Data governance always exists in some form within organizations, but it does not accomplish very much without data leadership.**

Data governance accomplishes little without data leadership, but data leadership doesn't accomplish *anything* without data governance (which, fortunately for us, always exists in some form). And we *will* get more done with data leadership if we have competent data governance.

We can think of data governance as a necessary, but insufficient, building block of data leadership. We should also understand that it is likely that our organizations are starting with some amount of formalized data governance, whereas it is far less likely that they already have a focused data leadership program in place.

DATA LEADERSHIP FOR DATA GOVERNANCE

It is reasonable that we spend a little time going through data governance fundamentals, and even for the seasoned pros out there, this section may have a slightly different perspective from the norm. To get data governance right, we must start at the beginning by asking what is triggering the call for data governance in an organization. First, let's think about banks.

Banks are great. You give them your money, and then they give it back when you need it. Some pay you a few cents a month for the privilege, while others make you pay them to manage your money. Doesn't that sound like a great business model? Having people pay you to watch their money? How does any bank ever go out of business?

The banking industry has attracted some unwanted attention related to fraud and mortgage-backed securities, among other crises over the years, and these have resulted in a healthy amount of regulation. Legislation like Dodd–Frank and Sarbanes–Oxley in the United States has added a fair amount of complexity to how banks must operate and, importantly, outlined some of the controls that must exist to protect the stability of the banking system. One of these controls is that banks must have data governance. Though the preceding sentence is not directly quoting the regulation, the lack of precision is about the same.

Regulators are typically not deep experts in the data space, but someone suggested including data governance, and the provision sounded good to them at the time. I met one of these regulators at a conference once, and I asked him how they create these regulations. He glanced over his shoulders, leaned toward me slightly, and softly said that they write something intentionally vague but with some directional guidance and then wait to see how the companies react. When the regulators see something they like, they point to it and tell others to do it that way too!

This blew my mind, but after thinking about it for a while, it makes perfect sense, and thus regulatory mandates like this are one way data governance gets off the ground. When a governing body tells us that we must comply with confusing mandates or there will be fines or other penalties, our executives will usually support efforts to comply.

....

Regulatory origins for data governance are a common—but dangerous—way to spearhead data governance efforts.

....

Regulation-inspired data governance initiatives tend to focus on compliance above all else and never amount to more than a necessary cost of doing business. These will tend to focus on checking the right boxes and assigning people to roles and definitions to terms, and they are largely exercises in satisfying regulators who don't even understand it all in the first place. People involved feel obligated to do things, but their hearts are not in it, and the entire program is considered a necessary evil. Data governance can be so much more!

Data governance should not exist simply to go through the motions for regulatory purposes. Data governance must help the organization operate better through more effective use of data.

This is the other origin story for data governance: when it is created to drive data value and therefore promote data leadership. Linking data governance to data leadership still satisfies the regulatory hurdles but also creates momentum. This leads to an easier program to keep running, as it is not simply a cost of doing business or a necessary evil. Even in regulated environments, creating data governance capabilities with an innovation mindset is the best way to maximize data value.

....

With data leadership–inspired data governance, executives can get excited about a positive ROI, and this enables us to align incentives and motivate everyone involved.

....

So now we understand what should be awfully similar motivations between starting data governance and promoting data leadership. One early step to making either one a reality is to get some support from the top. Executive sponsorship is a crucial component to creating something with enough scale to have a real impact. As we'll learn later, we do not need executive backing to demonstrate the potential of what we will do, but we sure will need their help to make it a full reality.

It's important to realize that executives typically exist in circumstances where positive gains are nice and helpful and *potentially* rewarding, but unexpected negative outcomes will be severely punished. Executives obviously want to support good ideas, but they also have a well-honed self-preservation instinct to distance themselves from failure. They also like to be associated with growth and new initiatives that have had no time to lose their luster, so while it is a necessary and laudable achievement to get top people to the data governance kickoff, what is truly impressive is when they have been continually involved a year later.

Despite what people on a lower rung may want to believe, executives are not stupid. We should give them a little credit: at least they were willing to stick their necks out far enough to recognize and support our data initiatives in the first place! But once things get going, most will delegate to us to keep things moving along while they turn their direct attention to other things. They simply do not have enough time in the day to be hands on with every function that rolls up to them.

GETTING DATA GOVERNANCE STARTED

What we haven't yet covered is the makeup of the data governance council or equivalent group in our organization. If we stack the data governance council with a bunch of high-ranking executives, we will have all the organizational firepower we need! The downside is that most senior folks are so busy they will rarely attend the meetings, and they are so far removed from the day-to-day interactions with data that they struggle with the detail demanded to perform effective data governance.

On the other hand, if we staff up our data governance council with a bunch of low-ranking folks who work with actual data all day, they will not have the organizational juice to make and enforce the necessary decisions made by data governance. So what should we do?

Both! Get a mix of folks with high-level strategic insights and those working more closely with data and customers on the front lines. The senior folks provide leadership and decision-making authority, and the lower-level folks have the detailed understanding to execute the tactical objectives effectively. Plus, it's exciting for a data analyst to serve on a committee with the VP of marketing, which means they will be highly motivated not to mess up. Even if the senior folks don't make all the meetings personally, if they remain engaged, the data governance organization can be successful.

The most successful data governance organizations tend to create a council with representation made up of both senior and lower ranks in the organization.

Now remember, just like everything in this book, we can establish guidelines, but the moment we go to apply them to an actual situation, things get complicated. It is imperative to work with what we have in our actual circumstances. All the general rules outlined here have trade-offs that may work in most situations but not necessarily the ones in which we find ourselves, so tread carefully!

That said, there are some truths that arguably apply in every circumstance. Like if we do not have executive support and sponsorship for data governance, we as data leaders need to cultivate it. Nothing is scarier than executives running companies without any appreciation or reliance on the value of data. If our business leaders take an ostrichlike head-in-the-sand approach and want to ignore everything about data, it might be a situation we can't fix, and we may want to find an organization that better shares our values.

If the executives appreciate that data has value but are not sure what to do about it, we should first buy them a copy of this book (or five, just to be safe!) and then start working together to create data value. Data governance activities will certainly be part of the answer and not necessarily a bad way for us to get some involvement from our business leadership.

So if we have compiled the leadership of our data governance organization and are ready to start doing something, watch out for the second trap that causes data governance to fail from the start: a focus on meetings.

When did meetings ever succeed as the place to get actual work done? Never! We cannot expect that data governance council meetings will magically become the first time we herded the cats into a windowless room, sometimes with snacks, and expect the outcome to be a tremendous data value creation.

Getting a group of low to senior executives together to talk about data on a regular basis is not the recipe for spectacular data success.

Please understand, data governance council meetings serve an important purpose in coordinating and clarification, but that purpose does not have enough critical mass from the first day in your data governance efforts. To start with meetings creates a top-heavy data governance effort that will eventually buckle under its own weight.

The solution is to begin the real work in the trenches. We will learn more specific techniques later, but if you want to get moving right now, follow these steps:

1. *Identify skills you know people will need to add data value in their roles but are currently lacking.* A good place to start is basic analytics and dashboarding tools. It can be Excel or something more sophisticated. Get people making basic visualizations and talking about what they think about the easy-to-reach data. This starts to slowly build your data culture.

2. *Gather the context of the data that exists.* This is what we call *metadata,* and it will start to lay the groundwork that data quality will be built on later. Data quality is how we know whether data can reliably be used for an intended purpose, and it is much easier to define than to achieve. When gathering and storing metadata, think about what might be useful to know in determining which data to use for various purposes.

3. *Find the struggling change initiatives.* Projects and programs that are funded and underway have something we won't have initially: a defined and agreed-on value proposition. Without data leadership, most initiatives will struggle with data. Ask project teams where they are running into difficulties (i.e., where tasks are more resource intensive than expected or where target dates are slipping). See if patterns can be spotted, and those will point the way toward great opportunities for data leadership.

As more data value opportunities become apparent, coordination and prioritization become worthwhile, and that's what will justify establishing a decision-making authority for data. Do note, once the data governance council is formed and begins to meet, we only have one or two meetings to solidify roles before people start losing interest and floating away. We must make sure that they have important, worthwhile things to do that give them a personal incentive to remain involved.

As the data governance organization starts to chalk up some wins, they will begin to drive their activities more independently. This momentum will allow us to take on more ambitious initiatives that will have ever-greater impacts on our organizations. We'll also be able to recruit more folks at all levels of the organization to jump on the bandwagon that is data governance.

As if "data governance" weren't a sexy enough name for what we do, we also have the role of "data custodian," or its marginally less awfully titled peer, the "data steward." Data custodians and data stewards are given responsibility to keep the data tidy. They may not make the decisions or determine the definitions of what the data means, but once the data governance organization does its part, the data custodians and data stewards make certain that the definitions and any other standards or policies are implemented clearly and consistently throughout the organization.

For our purposes, these titles can be used interchangeably, though I'm sure somewhere the person who came up with these names is going to be enraged, just like the folks who get upset when I play loosey-goosey by interchanging terms like "information management" and "data management."

For the rest of us, these roles may not seem so glamorous, even though one might argue that whenever we use data, we are also influencing its future use. The defined role of cleaning up data and ensuring it can be used elsewhere in an organization is an arduous, often thankless job. Most people are not clamoring to sign up for these responsibilities, and for good reason which is a big reason why data governance is often doomed from the start.

If we start data governance by asking people to help us, we are implying that our needs are more important than theirs.

People want to help one another, especially within organizations, but when they see little personal gain from the work they do on behalf of someone else, they will not stay motivated. Data governance is often structured like a charity: please help us define and improve the quality of data so some future person's life will be a bit easier!

People typically mean well, but unless they are going to personally benefit from completing a project, it will be tough to get continuing support for the long term. Those being asked to help will quickly find the path of least resistance, which is to do just enough to not get yelled at. They will mostly stay under the radar, but this will weaken the foundation of our data governance efforts and ultimately erode participation until data governance just fades away completely. Sound familiar?

SUSTAINING DATA GOVERNANCE

Experience shows us that even under the best of circumstances, building lasting data governance is tough, but this unbalanced approach to data governance further hurts our chances for success. We must create an environment where our chances are maximized.

I prefer a bridge-builder analogy for a lot of what we do with data. Data people help connect the different areas and needs of a business by building data and technology "bridges" between them. Data people don't necessary understand all the ins and outs of the business traffic traversing the bridge, but we sure know how to build the bridges. Bad data governance often tries to build every bridge that can possibly be built, just in case somebody wants to drive over it someday. If we were talking about real bridges, nobody would ever even attempt that (not even California!). Of course a build-every-conceivable-bridge program is going to fail spectacularly!

So if the usual approach won't work, what should we do instead? We should focus on data value. You knew I was going to say that, didn't you?

Who cares about data governance? It is simply a means to an end. That end is data value, as we defined at the start of this book.

We don't need data governance programs. We need data leadership programs that drive data value. We need to teach our businesses to use data to improve what they do.

Will we sneak some data governance in alongside data leadership? Absolutely. Executing data governance productively is more important than ever, but it must be done in the context of something that matters to people who would never willingly sign up for something called "data governance."

When we focus on data value first, we can identify how any individual might stand to gain by performing a data steward-ship role. We can then motivate them to stay involved using the best motivator around: their own self-interest!

The benefit of this approach cannot be overstated. One of the most common patterns of failing data governance efforts is focusing on persuading others to help *us* achieve *our* goals. We need to flip that around: data governance must exist to help *others* achieve *their* goals.

When we focus our approach to data governance on how we can help others instead of how others can help us, we will find ways to connect to the business that would otherwise never be found.

Remember the value of data—it is all rooted in the ability to measurably improve business outcomes. The more you serve to help a business achieve its objectives faster or help calibrate already-in-progress initiatives, the more momentum you can build to take on the transformative opportunities that data analytics will uncover.

Earlier in this chapter, we talked about how many organizations currently have data governance, regardless of whether they actively manage it. What we must also recognize is even the most competent data governance organizations will have some aspects of data they are not actively managing. Not only is this okay, but it is also necessary. We won't be able to control it all, and if we try, we're simply going to create a terrible bottleneck that stifles productivity and innovation.

While addressing the failures of "traditional" data governance warrants the additional focus of this chapter, later we will reframe data governance in the context of creating data value as part of a balanced data leadership approach, and this is exactly where data governance belongs.

....

We need to weave data leadership into an existing business to create data-driven change without being so disruptive that it hurts more than it helps.

....

Organizations need to crawl with data before they run and eventually fly. Some businesses out there do not have much of an existing relationship with data today, so you'll need to start slowly. There is a time and place for massive, rapid changes, but those tend to come with collateral damage. Years ago, when Netflix sold their DVDs in the mail business in favor of a nascent streaming content business model, people thought they were nuts! Some of you just looked up what a DVD is, didn't you? Point made.

Our customers have a limit to how much change they can handle at one time. They can be fickle, and sometimes they can be wrong, and other times they are right. Whatever shall we do? We must pick our spots, focus on data value, and get working on things that deliver the most of it.

5

STOP *TALKING* ABOUT WORKING... AND START WORKING

MOVE QUICKLY AND GATHER MORE DATA

Anyone fortunate enough to have children or spend much time around them will be familiar with an occasional accident. This will either destroy something Daddy or Mommy loves or cause some easily avoidable injury to their siblings or to themselves. On questioning, the perpetrator will inevitably respond, "But I didn't *mean* to!"

What kids and CEOs sometimes seem not to understand is that actions have consequences. Our intentions only matter when selecting and performing actions, but they are no longer relevant when consequences have already occurred. In business and in life, we will be judged on outcomes alone—that and how much people like working with us.

Perhaps you are interested in defending an approach that may not work out quite as well as you hope. Or you are looking for more quantifiable evidence that your performance is as spectacular as you believe. Data will help in either of these use cases and many, many more.

Data provides transparency between cause and effect—it brings us closer to the truth. That's why it is so upsetting when people choose to ignore data. Those folks looking to avoid truth will not be reading this, and they are going to find it harder and harder to remain relevant in a quickening world. So if you are on board with the relevance and potential of data analytics, what do you do first?

Answer: Anything other than have a meeting.

....

Great ideas never implemented accomplish nothing, far less than good ideas implemented well.

....

Momentum is built through motion and mass. Data governance standards and policies have plenty of substance, but the motion part comes from acting. As we mentioned in the last chapter, data leadership is how we'll build that motion, and in the next chapter, we will introduce the data leadership framework and begin to peel back the complexity of everything organizations can do to get the most from data.

We know we want to take action to make real differences, and we will cover the many disciplines necessary to accomplish all we want to achieve. These are not enough, however, to ensure lasting data success.

Actively building and managing momentum is paramount if we hope to keep data efforts alive. We cannot expect an if-you-build-it-they-will-come approach to succeed for any amount of time. People are fickle and will not blindly serve the common good for long if those energies fail to give them something back.

By actively solving for this challenge, we can give our efforts the chance of long-term success.

But there is a gap between completely organic, unmanaged data governance and the more robust data leadership framework that has a lot going on. What we need is something that helps get us started and moving along well enough to kick things into higher gear. Fortunately, we have such a something.

THE SIMPLE VIRTUOUS CYCLE: THE ENGINE OF DATA LEADERSHIP

The simple virtuous cycle reduces the complex topic of creating data value into its smallest, most atomic form. This cycle can be found inside most business processes, with multiple instances of varying scales working in harmony. As the world around us gets ever more complex with new technologies and greater demands for data, we can distill them into this foundational cycle:

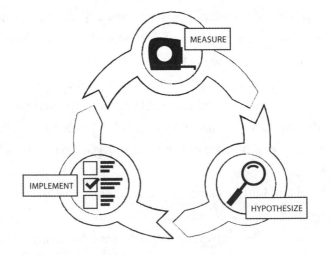

The Simple Virtuous Cycle

Everything we want to do in the world of data can follow this simple pattern:

1. *Measure:* Establish a baseline, and understand the complexities of the situation. In many circumstances, this gets skipped completely. Measuring can feel so difficult, and there is an unavoidable sense of vulnerability when starting to be more quantitative. But consider the alternative: we don't measure and have no idea which actions are working and which changes we should make! Who's feeling vulnerable now? Bottom line, get measuring!

2. *Hypothesize:* Compile and quantify potential actions and their range of likely outcomes. Most of the time today, people advocate for what they intuitively feel is best and just run with it. Instead, by taking a more quantitative approach rooted in data value, we miss fewer good opportunities and make the most of limited resources.

3. *Implement:* Carry out the most compelling actions we've arrived at from steps 1 and 2. As measurements are a crucial part of the simple virtuous cycle, any changes should drive both data value and accommodate future measurements and improvement cycles. Often people are so focused on planned deliverables that they fail to prepare for future cycle iterations.

The simple virtuous cycle can operate at large and small scales, but when starting out, it is advantageous to try to make the cycles as small as possible. Think simple measurements, a few ideas for change, followed by easy implementations.

Remember, this is about building momentum as much as it is about optimizing outcomes.

Why does this flywheel work? It keeps us focused on delivering data value as fast as possible. We must keep completing the cycle of value delivery to propel our organization forward. Think of this cycle as the wheels of a car spinning. Large efforts are akin to large wheels, taking longer to complete each revolution. At speed, large wheels may operate more efficiently by covering more ground with each revolution, but they are more costly to build and take more effort to get spinning in the first place.

Since a car can't practically change its wheel sizes, transmissions exist to change the gearing so that the engine's power can accelerate a car going different speeds. The more gears a transmission has, the more it can fine-tune power delivery. A continuously variable transmission (CVT) effectively does so without limit. The output of a CVT is like infinite variations of wheel sizes on a fixed axle.

This is why we start with small iterations that can get going with limited effort and resources. In data leadership, we can always increase the size of the efforts over time as things get moving, just like a CVT in an automobile does. The simple virtuous cycle similarly creates a self-reinforcing system that gets stronger (and bigger) as time goes on. When we have enough momentum, the full-fledged data leadership framework will help us get wherever we want to go.

The other reason to start with small improvements is that we do not need any specific domain expertise to get going. Yes, an advanced knowledge of data quality theory will help us implement a robust data quality scoring and remediation program at some point, but today we might know that the sales quantities that the finance department is using are not reconciling to the totals from operations. Why not dive into that one right now? Quantifying the high-level ROI should take about five seconds, and we will learn something new along the way too!

....

We must constantly remind ourselves to spend less time talking about working and more time *actually* working.

....

We won't change anything by talking about working. It is only by putting ourselves in motion that we can hope to transform our organizations. This also means that to be successful, we will need to get people to change their behaviors.

INTENTIONS ARE DIFFERENT FROM OUTCOMES

To make things a little more complicated, simply changing peoples' behaviors is not enough to create data value. Effort is not the same thing as results. This seems obvious, but do not dismiss it. Perhaps more than any other cause, time is wasted by "busy" people who foolishly believe that what they are doing matters. Despite having the best intentions, even the most talented among us can create negative value by focusing on the wrong things.

This is exemplified in how I came to have one of my most cherished office treasures: an autographed 2005 World Series baseball.

Every organization has little things about their culture that makes the place unique. At one of my former employers, this took the form of people having balls that they would toss around or bounce against the walls. This could be mildly distracting, but mostly it was a little bit of simple stress relief in an intense place.

The balls that people owned seemed to be reflections of their personalities or what they cared about. Some had special meaning, and others were nothing more than the left-behinds of the person who used to have the office. One person had a racquetball that he would bounce against the wall to relieve stress, and another had a football that they'd flip up in the air to themselves or toss to another person while solving the world's problems.

I saw this pattern, and because I wanted to fit in, I decided that I too should bring in a ball. Since I'm a White Sox fan and I like to overthink even the simplest of decisions, I thought it might be fun to have a ball from the 2005 World Series, in which my beloved White Sox had their moment of glory by winning it all for the only time in my lifetime.

Seeing as it was now over a decade later, I figured that would be the right mix of novelty and personal meaning to send the right message (beyond the one that I'm a data geek with a tendency to overanalyze everything).

At the time, I did not own a 2005 World Series baseball, so I took to the internet to see what options I might have. A cursory evaluation on Amazon and eBay showed me what I would likely need to spend. If I wanted a plain, non-game-used baseball with the 2005 logo, it was running about fifty dollars. Game-used or autographed balls went up from there. A real treasure like a Paul Konerko–signed ball was in the $350 range, and a ball signed by the entire team got obscene—into four figures.

My "brilliant" idea appeared to be unrealistic. I mean, there was no way I was spending even fifty dollars for this silly exercise. But I did think it would be fun to own a 2005 World Series ball, so I went back to the internet one last time to see if I could find something, anything, that would be less expensive.

That was when I stumbled on it: an authentic 2005 World Series ball for only twenty dollars. And autographed, no less!

I thought it was a typo in the listing at first, but on closer scrutiny, I realized what was going on. This ball was listed by a sports memorabilia store that traded mostly in autographed items and other interesting sports stuff that collectors pay lots of money to acquire. Everything was supply and demand based, and the prices varied wildly based on how much people were willing to pay.

This was the reason the autographed ball was worth twenty dollars in the market: it was signed by a Houston Astros rookie named Chris Burke. He ended up in the major leagues only for a handful of years, and his career ended in 2009. Not only did Houston lose the World Series in question, but this ball was signed by a person who most casual baseball fans would not recognize a decade later.

The Chris Burke–autographed 2005 World Series baseball may have been the best twenty dollars I've ever spent. Not only did I get the ball I knew I wanted, marred slightly by a little bit of blue ink, but I also received a bit of wisdom that continues to guide me today:

Adding energy to something is not the same as adding value.

When Chris Burke signed that ball in 2005, he certainly did not intend to decrease its market value by 60 percent. He reasonably thought that by scribbling on that ball, he'd be giving somebody a fine memento of a special event. Oh boy, did he ever!

Even today, that ball sits on my desk, and I often glance over at it or pick it up and toss it around while on calls or otherwise pondering some data-related challenge. It reminds me to carefully consider how my actions will result in real value and not cause unintended negative outcomes.

Too few of our efforts are calibrated cautiously enough. It's not uncommon to see pointless meetings being held, business glossaries going unused, standards and policies being ignored, or entire efforts stalling due to ineffectiveness. How many organizations roll out an entire new platform without proper training for staff and then are dismayed when it doesn't get the usage it should?

We are all surrounded by folks who equate being busy with being productive, and that is simply foolish. We each must force ourselves to think about the ball we are signing in our own work and how all our efforts in the data world are dependent on one another.

....

Putting in effort is no guarantee of creating positive value—in data, business, or *baseballs*.

....

After all, the reason my autographed ball was worth so much less had nothing to do with how Chris Burke signs a baseball. By all measures, he has a perfectly fine signature—every bit as nice as Konerko's. The value of sports memorabilia derives from the outcomes achieved on the field, often the results of the energies expended throughout an entire career. It has nothing to do with the signature itself.

I did not know anything about Chris Burke before finding that ball. I am sure this is not the outcome he expected to create when signing it. Certainly, he did not predict that it would eventually become one of the most prized possessions of a White Sox fan. Playing several years of major-league baseball is no failure by any measure.

But every day when I sit down in my office to try to improve businesses with data, I see that ball perched on my desk. And every day, it reminds me of an important lesson that guides everything that I do: don't be Chris Burke, meaning "try not to accidentally decrease value through my actions despite having good intentions." This resolves to the convenient and easy-to-remember acronym TNADVTMADHGI. Or just remember "Don't be Chris Burke" and recall this story.

When we find ourselves in a Chris Burke–like situation, we should try to calibrate our behavior so we are more likely to create real value in the end. And if you are *literally* Chris Burke, sorry for using you as a cautionary tale in a data book, and thanks for the autograph!

DATA LEADERSHIP IS NOT REALLY ABOUT DATA AT ALL

Data leadership hasn't really been addressed before in the way we are talking about it in this book: we are trying to change people's behaviors while acknowledging that it is really challenging to change people's behaviors. It doesn't even matter if it is our customers', our company's, or even our own behavior. Creating data value has more to do with people than data.

Data leadership is not about data at all. It is about changing people's behavior.

We know a few truths about people:

1. **People resist change.**
2. **People are watching out for themselves above all else.**
3. **Even if doing something would benefit them, see point 1.**

Does that sound like a party we want to attend? It seems like a recipe for disaster, and that's exactly what happens when people try to do data by coming in guns blazing with a bunch of meetings alongside grandiose ambitions of changing everything! Of course, it is doomed to failure. Do we expect fundamental human nature to step aside just because data is important? Do we think we're going to make a difference by getting some people in a room to argue about who our customer is?

We need to be much more thoughtful about how we engage, especially in the early days of fostering data leadership. We must operate in the shadows of our organizations, doing good for the sake of doing good and building capabilities that are useful immediately for people just trying to get their normal stuff done.

One particularly useful approach to achieving this is a

management philosophy called "servant leadership." Servant leadership is a term that is what it says it is (data management folks take note!). Servant leaders help their teams succeed by removing anything that blocks them from completing their tasks. Whether reaching out to the business for requirements clarifications, procuring new technical tools, or jumping in to lend some specific expertise, servant leaders stop at nothing to support their teams. Data leaders must approach our roles similarly.

Data leaders have at least one shared goal with everyone we encounter: to create data value.

We must remove the blockers that stand in the way of progress and help that value become realized.

It does not even need to be complicated. By leveraging the simple virtuous cycle, it can be as easy as this:

- **Wake up.**
- **Create data value (measure, hypothesize, implement).**
- **Go to sleep, excited to do it again tomorrow!**

But doesn't that oversimplify it a bit? Yep, but not as much as it might seem at first. We as people, especially those of us interested in data and technology, tend to overcomplicate things. The blockers we encounter may come from organizational resistance, a "not my job" mentality, fear of change, lack of technology tools, or good ol' laziness.

So what? We have already established that the futures of our businesses are on the line, and we are the keys that will unlock data value. If there were no blockers, people would have fixed all this already, and we wouldn't have such awesome opportunities in front of us. When faced with the incredible potential of transforming our businesses, none of the blockers out there should remain for long.

We understand what creates data value, how it is measured, and why trying to go too big initially is a recipe for disaster. If we look for the little ways to create business outcome improvements, we will build toward more substantial results.

If we are still feeling a little leery about stepping into the spotlight as a data leader, think about the worst-case scenario: our passion about changing the world, or at least our businesses, with data value falls on completely deaf ears, and the rest of our company's leadership has no interest in improving business outcomes. Beyond not supporting us, they are so averse to challenging the status quo that they fire us. What happens then?

First, the chances of that are incredibly low, but let's explore, since it is always a good idea to explore border conditions. There are far too many organizations out there desperately trying to find a way to use data better. Do not waste your time with one that you need to convince that data is important. Today the idea of working for a data-ignorant company is like working for a company that refuses to let people access the internet. Do they still use paper ledgers for accounting too? Slide rules? Horse-drawn carriages?

The bottom line is that creating real data value is hard enough to get right in an organization that "gets it" and fully supports our data endeavors. Let's not waste our time working for those organizations that are already toast, and make no mistake, if they haven't figured out by now that data is valuable, they are already too far gone.

It is not too late for an organization that realizes data is valuable, wants to do something about it, but has no idea what to do, but there is no time left to waste.

The fact is that *most* organizations today believe data is valuable, so there is certainly still hope for them. Especially since they have us. When we put our good intentions to work by using an effective framework, we can accomplish anything. Fortunately for us, and our organizations, the next part of this book provides exactly that.

PART 2

THE DATA LEADERSHIP FRAMEWORK

PART 2

DATA LOADING AND

FRAMEWORKS

6

INTRODUCING THE DATA LEADERSHIP FRAMEWORK

WHY THE DATA LEADERSHIP FRAMEWORK

We attend data management conferences and find no executives. We attend technology conferences and find no data people. Executives have their own secret conferences somewhere only for them. This is no surprise, as there is nothing more human than breaking ourselves off into little groups to talk about stuff.

We've spent decades breaking our companies into subsets of functional expertise, and we have reinforced these divisions by disincentivizing folks from working together. For most corporate positions, our compensation structures tend to focus on our individual activities instead of the actual impact we have on the business. How many bonuses are determined by how well the technology team impacted operational efficiencies? Too few.

This isn't because we want our people to have a minimal impact on the business with what they do all day. It is because measuring that contribution is hard. And if measuring it is hard, then creating incentives around it is harder, and then coaching folks' behaviors to make it happen becomes downright dismal. We'd rather just tell people to knock out some widgets and call it a day.

Fortunately, the intrepid data leader will not back down from this kind of challenge. We recognize that the more difficult path will lead us to our greater potential and that the pain of creating better incentive structures is just one of the many side effects of transforming our businesses to become data driven.

It's like exercise: we may feel sore after a workout, but we know what we did will ultimately be good for our health. Organizational healthiness sounds like it would be a great idea to shoot for, but it is a nebulous metric to define. Which numbers would go into that?

Data leadership can't be prescribed. It is a means of assessing situations, determining actions, and implementing them well.

Plenty of companies make tremendous profit, but so did Sears, until it didn't. Growth could be another subcomponent of organizational healthiness, but then you look back at a company like Enron, which had a trajectory like the model rocket I built in high school that I strapped eight extra engines onto. Like Enron, my rocket was remarkably fast and largely unstable, and it caused a bit of a fire when it crashed.

The data leadership framework (DLF) was born from these premises:

- To succeed in the face of improving competition, we must continually become better at what we do.
- Data will help us determine how to optimize our limited resources in pursuit of improvements.
- Organizations today are rampantly ineffective in this pursuit. Data efforts that do exist are typically incomplete or overly subjective, or they miss some important aspect that, if addressed, would lead to much better outcomes.

The project-based change management approaches that companies typically use amplify their ineffectiveness. With finite timelines, resources, and scope, we compromise our ability to react to new information without laborious change requests or approval processes—if we are lucky enough to gain approval at all. The net result to project deliverables is cutting corners on things like testing, design, or robustness of the solution, but there is another hidden drawback that is even worse: if we optimize energies solely at the microscale (the project), we lose the ability to maximize impacts at the macroscale (the system).

> **To be successful with data-driven change, we must deliberately consider and act to optimize both individual and aggregated outcomes.**

This means that without well-coordinated data governance (macro) and project/program management (micro), our collections of individual projects will not result in the transformative impacts they were intended to have. While there are countless resources out there to help us get better at individual data management disciplines, there is a startling lack of resources to help us put them all together.

Similarly, there are thousands of books about building great businesses and developing leadership skills, but where's the beef? These leadership-focused works often fail to connect us to the daily grind of things like projects, operations, budgets, priorities, and varied expectations of stakeholders. People are trying to lead businesses at a time when data is crucial to success, but they still do not grasp foundational data management principles that are more important than ever!

The DLF expands on the simple virtuous cycle. It is designed to help us measure the overall transformative impact we're having and to help us correct course before we waste our efforts building something amazing at the wrong time or place.

Context is what makes data useful, and the DLF provides much-needed macroscale context to the detailed activities we spend most of our time doing.

....

Beyond just a process or a high-level strategy, the DLF includes targeted ways we can create more data value.

....

The data-oriented professional who wants to be successful must recognize that their fate is either to become a business leader or risk becoming irrelevant. Data leadership is really all about organizational change, which implies that the people involved will need to do something different. And this is true in the case of data value—until somebody takes action, any data-driven insights may be interesting but have only created potential, not actual, value.

Data folks love building data capabilities and may act like people merely get in the way, but people are the main way data realizes its potential value. To create data value, we need to address both the data and people sides of the equation, and we might as well throw in technology and process sides too. If we think of data and people as the nouns and technology and process as the verbs, these are the underpinnings of the entire DLF.

....

The DLF uses a data-focused nomenclature, but everything can be further distilled into people, process, data, and technology elements.

....

Data leadership is not the same as data management. Data management is focused on the functions of data, whereas data leadership focuses on improvements to the organization's outcomes. Data management seems much easier to fall back on—we can control data! The downside is that we won't really accomplish much until we connect the data capabilities to people.

Changing people's behavior doesn't work like putting data through a computer program. Programs are logical, unemotional, and reliable, and they do exactly as they are told. With people, if we get any of those attributes, we are lucky. No wonder data people love to focus on programming and computers—they are so much easier! But technology alone isn't the answer.

As we dive into the details, remember that each category overall and each discipline within the categories individually creates potential value. The category with the lowest data value creation capability limits the overall system's potential throughput. To create the category-level balance, it is reasonable to invest more or less energy in individual disciplines while even omitting some entirely at times.

DEFINING THE DATA LEADERSHIP FRAMEWORK

The DLF helps us achieve balance between the people, process, technology, and data capabilities we must create to maximize data value. First, we break down the universe of things we care about in data into five DLF categories:

1. *Access*: Prepare for Use
2. *Refine*: Build Potential
3. *Use*: Deliver Insights

4. *Impact*: Maximize Data Value
5. *Govern*: Scale Results

Each of these has a distinct and significant role, and with a balanced approach to address all of them, we will be able to create realized data value. The underlying hypothesis is that for the system to operate most effectively, these five categories must be in relative balance—that is, their overall output capacity must be of comparable strength to one another.

Within each of these DLF categories, we have four disciplines representing data and organizational change management functions where we can choose to devote energy (in the form of time, money, attention, etc.).

- **Access: Prepare for Use**
  - » **Compliance**
  - » **Architecture**
  - » **Wrangling**
  - » **Development**
- **Refine: Build Potential**
  - » **Context**
  - » **Quality**
  - » **Enrichment**
  - » **Curation**
- **Use: Deliver Insights**
  - » **Modeling**
  - » **Reporting**
  - » **Integration**
  - » **Operations**
- **Impact: Maximize Data Value**

- » Quantification
- » Data Science
- » Automation
- » Monetization
- Govern: Scale Results
  - » Strategy
  - » Change
  - » Adoption
  - » Stewardship

The four DLF disciplines in each DLF category do not need to be balanced within an individual category, but the disciplines should be used to compare and prioritize the allocation of finite resources toward the category-level goal.

This will become clearer as we progress through the categories and disciplines, but for now, know that the DLF categories are outcome oriented, and the DLF disciplines are input oriented. We cannot simply say, for example, we want to devote more resources to the refinement capabilities without at some point allocating them to specific efforts in quality, enrichment, etc. DLF disciplines are actionable, whereas the DLF categories represent the results of those actions.

ANOTHER WAY TO THINK ABOUT IT:

- DLF Categories
  - » Are conceptual-level topics
  - » Represent ways data evolves into value
  - » Are what we need to balance to maximize system throughput
- DLF Disciplines
  - » Are functional-level topics

» **Are where we direct energy to evolve data**
» **Are where we grow DLF categories and help keep them in balance**

The DLF is designed to be an aid in assessing existing environments, developing strategic approaches, and, most importantly, helping us know what to do next.

Before we get into the specifics of the DLF, it's also important to underscore that the DLF is merely a framework. It is intended to make complex subjects simpler for us to evaluate, prioritize, and compare with one another. The DLF does not contain specific answers so much as it helps us ask the right questions to determine what we need to do to create data value in our own unique context. It is most simply a starting point—one that we are all encouraged to use, adapt, and evolve to meet the needs of our individual organizations.

This brings up a good professional tip: always aim to know at least one more level of detail than the questions you expect to receive. It not only ensures you have the requisite mastery of a subject, but it also gives you the ability to answer questions confidently. There is a difference!

USING THE DATA LEADERSHIP FRAMEWORK

Just like few folks can find perfectly fitting formal wear off the rack, most companies will need some DLF tailoring before it fits like a glove. Whether adjusting some of the terminology, breaking it out into more or fewer components, or removing or recasting some parts entirely, it's all fair game. We're doing it too! If we let maximizing data value be our guide, nothing is off-limits. But before running off to change it, let's first spend some time understanding how we can use the DLF.

....

The DLF does not give us the answers, but it does give us some mighty useful questions.

....

First, think of the DLF as a collection of lights we will use to illuminate our organizations' challenges in maximizing data value. We can see the problems from every angle, and this clarity helps us assess what is really going on. We can see if we're starved for data or have plenty of data but few skills to analyze it. Maybe our data is too locked down, or maybe the data quality is such a mystery that people have no idea what they can reasonably do with it. Every organization has a unique mix of strengths and weaknesses, and the best approach to improve will depend on these and will also need to consider business strategy, available resources, and many other constraints.

While consultants get a fair amount of well-deserved criticism, the classic consultative approach works well with the DLF:

1. *Assess a situation:* Use the DLF categories and disciplines to think through various complexities of creating data value, noting areas of strength and weakness.
2. *Determine an optimal future state:* Consider changes in business activities and decisions that would drive the most impact to the business, could be informed by data, and can't currently be done.
3. *Evaluate the gaps between where we are now and where we want to be:* Consider which DLF categories are more capable than others, and prioritize which need the most help.
4. *Make change happen:* Improve the DLF disciplines that align to the DLF categories that need the most help.

While data value does not strictly flow in the order of access › refine › use › impact › govern, it is advisable to have more capabilities to the left of any arrow. So if your organization has a lot in the govern category but little in impact, then you likely need to put more energy into the impact category.

For example, imagine working for a business that makes a variety of snack cakes. Wouldn't that be wonderful? Though all the answers are delicious, we are considering whether to invest in reducing the time it takes to reconfigure the manufacturing line to make different products. After all, downtime means fewer cakes getting into hungry bellies, which means less revenue.

The challenge is we are unsure whether our changeover times are better or worse than our competitors or whether the improvements would be worth the investment. To understand, analyze, and optimize this situation, we can quickly assess and act using the DLF.

The DLF provides different lenses to help us break down a complicated situation. We can go one by one through each DLF discipline to individually consider how each pertains to our situation, use those to hypothesize our option set, and then choose which to implement. If this sounds like a more detailed version of the simple virtuous cycle, you are on the right track!

And while deep expertise in individual disciplines certainly helps, even a basic understanding can help us infer what we might need to do. Typically, we should do the best we can in breaking down the situation based on our own skills, and if we identify specific disciplines that feel especially relevant to the situation, we can always call internal or external experts to help fill in any knowledge gaps.

The output from our initial snack cake example might look like this:

- **Access: Prepare for Use**
  - » **Compliance**
    - Industry benchmark data source identified (procuring the benchmark data has nominal cost)
    - Existing manufacturing costs/times readily available in existing data warehouse extracts
    - No privacy or security concerns likely
  - » **Architecture**
    - Stand-alone Excel-based analysis
  - » **Wrangling**
    - Data fields in the file are separated by commas, and a

separate line within the file defines the data types (e.g., string, datetime, integer) for each data field

- Data analysts were consulted, and they express no concerns for the complexity of the ad hoc analysis

» **Development**

- N/R (not relevant for ad hoc analysis)

- **Refine: Build Potential**

  » **Context**

  - N/R

  » **Quality**

  - Sufficient for use based on anecdotal evidence

  » **Enrichment**

  - N/R

  » **Curation**

  - N/R

- **Use: Deliver Insights**

  » **Modeling**

  - Data analysts expressed no concerns

  » **Reporting**

  - Excel-based deliverable

  » **Integration**

  - N/R

  » **Operations**

  - N/R

- **Impact: Maximize Data Value**

  » **Quantification**

  - Compare current organization performance to industry norms

  » **Data Science**

  - N/R

- » **Automation**
  - – N/R
- » **Monetization**
  - – N/R
- **Govern: Scale Results**
  - » **Strategy**
    - – Consult with finance group. If organization is better than industry average or less than 15 percent worse, take no further action. If organization is more than 15 percent worse than industry, research improvement options.
  - » **Change**
    - – N/R
  - » **Adoption**
    - – N/R
  - » **Stewardship**
    - – N/R

The preceding is a simple example that would only take minutes to complete in the real world. Even in this basic case, however, by considering the different lenses represented by the DLF, we see items that would often be entirely overlooked in organizations trying to get better with data. The strategy discipline content is especially interesting, as it helps establish guidelines for the next steps even before the analysis occurs.

Think about how many times an analysis like this is completed and the only outcome is something like, "We're 5 percent worse than the industry average, so we should invest more time in figuring out what to do." Based on the example above, the moment the analysis returns 5 percent, it is already clear that the difference isn't significant enough to invest any more time.

It is typical to have disciplines that are not relevant to the *current decision* but will likely be needed if moving forward. Once this analysis is complete and the first decision is made, we can simplify the next iteration of the analysis to focus on *how* instead of *whether* we should act.

The purpose of the DLF categories is to corral the discrete DLF disciplines into a higher-level balance. DLF categories give us a way to prioritize the multiple things the discipline-level analysis tells us we should do into what we should do *next*.

. . . .

Category-level balance is almost always achieved through a wildly varying approach across DLF disciplines.

. . . .

Every organization does some things well and others not as well; the right allocation of energy to disciplines will depend much on those variables. Additionally, the allocations will change over time as new capabilities are introduced, and the efforts necessary to maintain these capabilities will be less than what it took to build them initially.

Data leaders strive to understand an entity's capabilities across the DLF categories and disciplines, guiding the prioritization and allocation of finite resources to maximize overall system balance and throughput.

Keep this mission in mind as we dive into the specifics, and remember, this is just the beginning. Each of the DLF disciplines represents a subject area where people devote entire careers. There are certainly plenty of additional resources to learn more, and we should try to gain, at minimum, a foundational understanding in each of them. The upcoming chapters are a start, but they represent more of a guide of what to study rather than providing enough depth to give us a fully informed perspective on their own.

7

ACCESS: PREPARE FOR USE

DATA THAT CAN'T BE USED WILL NEVER CREATE DATA VALUE

It all starts with access. Before we can create amazing capabilities that transform our businesses with data value, we need to connect to some data. This data can be sourced from countless places, both internal and external to our own organizations, using a variety of different technologies to facilitate these connections.

Typically, the most useful data for an organization to analyze is that which it creates directly through business operations. There are orders and transaction information, customer account records, products, part numbers, vendors, accounting journal entries, financial statements, HR and personnel information records—and these are just some obvious ones. Think about other things, like contracts, office leases, equipment, vehicles, insurance policies, compliance reports, and proprietary formulas and other trade secrets.

On top of those, we can add things like social media feeds, system logs, machinery sensors, graphical information systems (location-based) data, RFIDs, and I'm pretty sure those fancy door sensors that open with key cards create data too. The point is that we have a *ton* of data, and we still haven't gone beyond the data created inside our own companies! Using the DLF, we will be able to manage all the data we can find, and we will always be hungry for more!

Most organizations mess up internal data so badly that they should never go looking for more data from the outside.

These are unprecedented times after all. The world of data has never been more complex, with unbelievably capable technology tools and massive volumes larger than anything in the history of the world! The challenges we face as data professionals are so incredibly varied and expansive that it is monumentally difficult simply keeping up with the rapid pace of technology innovations that are enabling ever more data to be created and consumed!

And it will never be easier than it is right now.

By the time we can provide what is needed today, the world will change around us. The target will move, and we will still be behind where we need to be. We must therefore build extensible systems that can be adapted quickly to whatever the future may bring.

We do not have to predict the exact future to have systems that will accommodate it. We know the data will become more complex, bigger, faster, with new kinds of ever more granular precision, with businesses and potentially entire industries being built on organizations' abilities to act quickly on aggregations and patterns that today we cannot even identify. Cryptocurrencies, blockchains, self-driving cars—they are all going to continue to evolve, and the pace of change is only getting faster!

If we build our teams, our systems, and all our data capabilities based on *today's* needs, we will simply never catch up.

Before we get too far ahead of ourselves, as we mentioned at the start of this section, it all starts with access. And in the DLF, access starts with compliance. In today's world, anything we do with data must be done with an eye to appropriate use, privacy, and being good shepherds of the power data contains. Starting our journey with security reminds us of these responsibilities and gives us the appropriate context for the capabilities we build.

COMPLIANCE

As is the case with several of the DLF disciplines, we're taking a wide-angle view with these buckets. This one is called "compliance," which is how we determine what is permissible to do with data before we start moving it all over and changing business processes to create data value. This topic also encompasses data security, privacy, and anything where we are actively implementing the policies and standards coming from the govern category.

This area also tends to be overemphasized by people who specialize in it and largely ignored by those who do not. This must change, since compliance risks are only becoming higher and higher profile.

The 2017 Equifax breach settled this debate. When one of the pillars of the U.S. system of financial trust (i.e., personal credit) is compromised and their leadership bungles their response so spectacularly, the one thing we should immediately realize is that we never want that to be our company. We won't even discuss the casino that got hacked through a smart fish tank feeding system. Yes, that really happened.[1]

While here our focus is a bit more on *data* compliance and security, this data leadership discipline stretches across the technology landscape, including networks, general IT, the cloud, and devices (see *fish tank*, above). It also loosely contains security-adjacent topics like privacy, compliance, and contractual obligations. If somebody tells us we must do it or we should do it to protect our business interests, then it is within the scope of this DLF discipline.

Compliance ensures that people have access to the information they should and that people who should not have access don't.

Beyond that, compliance-related processes must reduce the likelihood that information is unintentionally shared with people who should not have it. These people may be bad actors, trying to break into data systems. It may even be the general public simply hanging out waiting for data to be dumped into their laps.

Security efforts, not unlike most data management functions, tend to be motivated by a few common patterns:

- A breach or other catastrophe has already occurred.
- A regulatory/compliance/audit finding has identified nonconformance or a lack of competency.
- An executive read something that got them worked up. This is a surprisingly frequent cause of major corporate initiatives.
- A well-reasoned business strategy has recognized that valuable data assets should be treated appropriately.

It may be clear by the wording, but my preference is that we be strategically motivated to do these things, but in real-world circumstances, the preceding list is ordered from most likely to least likely in what will bring compliance to the top of your to-do list.

Recall that the DLF has five different categories each composed of four different disciplines to think about and balance our meager resources across. Each of them is going to feel important when we think about them individually. We must do our best to figure out at any moment in time which ones are going to help balance the categories and create the most realized data value in the end.

Security is especially interesting when put in this context. When we consider the three forces of data value (increasing revenue, decreasing costs, managing risks), compliance is going to primarily help manage risk. If we do compliance well, we will probably avoid losing a lot of money due to not having it, but even if we do compliance well, it will never remove all the risks of data. We do not want to do compliance at the expense of everything else in the DLF, but if we don't at least establish some core capabilities, we will be incurring an outsized amount of unnecessary risk.

We must admit, it's inconvenient and annoying to have to deal with compliance or security. That's why nobody likes the CISO (chief information security officer), always running around, talking about how the sky is falling and we are all doomed. This is a tough life. It's not that what the CISO says is wrong or unimportant (in fact, we just explained why it is super important). It is simply that CISOs often present one-sided arguments about what we *shouldn't* do, *can't* do, or *aren't allowed* to do without considering that businesses don't become successful by *not* doing things.

Organizations must complement their value-creating activities with negative-value-avoiding activities to end up with the most data value.

This brings us back to data leaders. We need to be mindful of compliance constraints as we develop all the other capabilities to create data value. These seemingly opposed forces are hard for us to do full justice to, as they require fundamentally different mindsets. Now if only we could find an ally who would help propel our data leadership efforts with this world of compliance and security. Perhaps it may be someone having trouble connecting their work to business value and who may be underappreciated in the organization...

Aha! We could help the CISO (or equivalent position in the organization)! If nobody like that exists, we could build a business case for getting somebody into that role. If an organization fights the need for compliance after Equifax (or the casino fish tank story), we have big problems! If I found myself in that situation, I'd appeal directly to the CEO, but if that didn't work, it might be time to find work at an organization that actually wants to survive in today's data-driven world.

But sadly, deciding to invest energy in compliance is not an impressive win. We have not actually done anything to build compliance yet. We may reasonably start with identifying areas of risk, crafting some policies, establishing acceptable uses, and getting some people to agree that those are good ideas. Again, it's good talking about important things, but nothing real has happened.

We then need to implement the ideas. With our new friend the CISO, additional support from others in IT, buy-in from the business (which is willing to change some of its ways for the benefits of safety), a bit of time, plus ability to bridge any skills gaps—which there always are—if we can develop all these things, we can begin to implement some functional security capabilities that will help us manage data-related risk in our business.

Seems like a lot of work, right? Yeah, it is. All this is a lot of work. It will be easy to burn out our team or wear out our welcome if we're not careful. Heck, it's easy to do that even if we are careful. But if we get it right and can manage the balancing act of data leadership, the impact to our businesses will be transformational!

As we move into review of other disciplines and the need to maintain balance throughout the categories, the following is a good rule of thumb to follow: in the beginning of our data leadership journey, we should do a little of many things, a lot of a few things, and one thing to become world class. This becomes a promise of what is possible.

Becoming excellent at one thing builds confidence that we can become great at anything.

Security is an essential place to spend some time, but it is probably not the place most of us should try to become world class (apologies to the CISOs out there). Risk mitigation alone is not strong enough to prioritize compliance over other data leadership disciplines. That being the rule, of course there are exceptions.

If we are in the credit-reporting business or some other industry of such high trust where a data breach would likely result in bankruptcy, security may well be the place to become world class . Consumer-facing financial institutions, health-care organizations with private health information, or defense-related companies may well have compliance at or near the top of their priorities. With regulatory developments like HIPAA and the European General Data Protection Regulation (GDPR), the stakes are getting ever higher.

Compliance and security competency is essential for all

businesses, but doing it alone at the expense of all the other data leadership disciplines would be silly. If our businesses fail because they could not use data to create value, there's nothing to protect. Balance, baby—it's everything!

ARCHITECTURE

"Architecture," from a data perspective, has become an interesting term these days. It used to be *relatively* simple*: at the center of our data world, we had a big relational data warehouse with a data model that reflected a refactoring of the contents of various data sources to create a form that is generally intuitive for a wide variety of data consumers. Wait—that's not simple!

Let's try this again.

Architecture, specifically of the data persuasion, used to be simpler than it is today. First, operational systems would create data by performing core business functions. These are things like point-of-sale, customer account management, or inventory systems. Typically, operational reporting, analyzing data from one system at a time, was done within the operational systems themselves, as they were structured specifically to work with the creation and analysis of data from that one system.

Then the data was sent over from all the operational systems to a central location, commonly a data warehouse. This consolidated location was where cross-system data analysis was performed, identifying how data from multiple systems combines to inform us about the entire business. Reports, interactive dashboards, or other data-driven outputs would flow outward from the data warehouse.

---

* Get it? Data jokes are the best!

This pattern worked well for a long time, as the most important data to any organization is the data created by the execution of its core business processes. This is still true and is why data warehouses are still central to many organizations' data efforts. The downside, though, is that data warehouses rely on rigid models that must be developed before the data can be populated. Also, future enhancements can be difficult, as the heavy number of dependencies can make evolving a data warehouse feel like a complicated surgery of opening up its body and moving a bunch of innards around. It's not as gross as it sounds, but it is just as complicated.

Given that the amount of data we're dealing with in our organizations has exploded in recent years, the rigid data warehouse structures simply can't keep pace anymore. We need to support much more rapid changes while having less centralized control over the change. That's not to say we shouldn't be interested or have a role, but we can't put big rigid architectures at the center anymore.

If everyone is doing data analytics and trying to create data value, centralizing data or change controls will create bottlenecks that slow everyone down. This is bad.

Today, because data has grown so much and has become so central to business operations, the architecture discipline has grown to cover more ground. *Data* architecture has now evolved to cover some of the same ground as traditional *enterprise* architecture. Enterprise architecture is how a (typically larger) organization ensures that all change efforts fit together in a way that benefits the overall organization in addition to smaller areas within the organization.

An example would be having a standard laptop vendor for everyone in a company. The build process, replacement part inventory, service training, etc. would all benefit from the consistency more than each person would benefit from being able to choose whichever brand of laptop they wanted.

In the context of data architecture, we encounter a similar pattern. To create the beneficial consistencies across organizational data, a data architect is tasked with figuring out where to prescribe standards and common tools and processes and where to let people using data do what they want. After all, too much restriction leads to bottlenecks, which creates less data value.

Technology systems are all data driven, and a data architect needs to curate information flows in much more dynamic ways than we did in the olden times of the early 2000s. We are far removed from the days of connecting to a few data sources, modeling them into a dimensional model, knocking out a few data movements and transformations, and then hitting the golf course. Today's data architects often have visibility and responsibility across an entire organization.

In the spirit of managing complexity through simplification, why bother with <choose-any-kind> architecture at all? With everything converging, the roles of data architect, systems architect, enterprise architect, infrastructure architect, etc. cease to need the differentiation they once did.

Granted, there's still the confusion with architects who build buildings and whatnot, but what are they doing worried about all this data stuff? Oh yeah, their industry has been completely transformed by data and technology too! Let's go get some engineers with unclear roles and we can all be confused about titles together! Call the business analysts too! Nah, those are problems for a different day. Hopefully the context in our conversations can help us sort it all out.

The point here is that not only are the systems that create and use data becoming more complex, but today's data consumers are also more sophisticated; they are developing regression analyses and predictive analytics or demanding real-time interactive dashboards that are device agnostic. If we don't get some architecture in here quick, we're going to have problems!

....

The tools we have now can handle an incredible amount of data throughput, and it is up to us to fill those pipes with good stuff!

....

Fortunately, the data providers and sourcing options are just as powerful. Many organizations have become data service providers, happily willing to provide us whatever we can imagine, for a fee. Classic data service businesses like Dun & Bradstreet made their name compiling basic location and industry information about all businesses, and Michael Bloomberg famously made his fortune selling research and pricing data through his Bloomberg Terminal system for the financial industry. Even for us cheapskates, there are a tremendous number of free and open data sources available. If you want to do something like weather-trend sales analysis, for example, the amount of free weather data available out there will blow your mind!

At this point, we've covered the bookends of data consumers and producers, but what about the operational systems inside our businesses? All these internally created data sources we talked about earlier are also driven and enhanced by data. The architects need to get these systems to play nicely to share their information effectively, all the while acting in accordance with data governance and security policies. There are also data feedback loops that are created to serve operational processes within the overall data value chain, and architects are involved with it all!

Architecture is no longer just about the data warehouse that needs to serve up information to some analysts. Architectures are everywhere throughout our businesses.

It's the architects who weave this tapestry of capabilities together and ensure that the data can flow as needed. In addition to the substantial amount of work in architecture alone, most architects get pulled into a dozen other areas covered by the DLF.

So where does architecture fit in priority-wise? Well, everybody needs at least a little bit to make anything work with data value, so it must be on the radar to get some attention. The funny thing is that we probably have a lot of it already. It just may have been built haphazardly with no coordination and is now causing a bunch of problems with sharing information.

Sounds a lot like data governance when we think about it. The fact is that architecture *is* a lot like data governance in that both disciplines create structures and processes for information to flow. The difference is that data governance does it with a focus on the people impacting the data flows through business process, and architecture concerns itself more with the technology systems and databases that impact the physical data movements and storage.

The wrong way of thinking about these disciplines is to plan on, for example, doing a big, isolated architecture project to give this access DLF category a boost. It is more appropriate to think of these DLF disciplines as different colored lights that, when combined correctly, illuminate truth without bias. This may be the closest analogy to what we are trying to achieve.

Resource limitations, which we all have, mean that we can never afford to do anything to the absolute maximum, as we would consume too many resources to justify the minimal improvements as we approach those limits. We should instead do enough to keep our data capabilities across everything at roughly similar levels. It is this balance that creates a stable foundation from which to grow sustainably.

Regardless of our preferred metaphor, architecture is a deep bucket, and because it is influenced so much by technology, it changes constantly. Architects will know relational databases and be fluent in SQL pretty much always. If an architect doesn't at least know SQL, it is going to be difficult to be good at the job. SQL skills are necessary but insufficient to become exceptional at the data side of architecture.

Great architects understand how the business is likely to change and create real value from interactions with the architecture.

Architects will not necessarily need to have deep, heartfelt conversations directly with the business on a regular basis, but they will need to be able to grasp the business enough to make independent and accurate determinations about design and technology. We cannot afford to slow down the process by spoon-feeding architects everything they need to consider as they design what needs to be done.

Finally, architects must be self-motivated and push to get things built at all costs. Passive architects are going to fail us every time. If we are performing the architecture role ourselves as data leadership advocates, it may be a fine approach if we possess all the technical and leadership skills to do the job, but we must recognize that we will need some extra help on other specific areas if our individual responsibilities are spread across many other data leadership disciplines. Even in small companies, single individuals can rarely cover all the disciplines in the DLF, and even the rare folks with the skills will not have enough time to do them all well.

Architecture is no doubt an important consideration in any organization, but like many other design activities, it tends to fall into the "talking about working" trap. Having some foundational architecture directives in place may be all we need to start getting our hands dirty and start building our data-driven future. And nothing dirties the hands quite like wrangling.

WRANGLING

"Data wrangling" as a name chosen to describe something in the data management space is about as good as it gets when it comes to jargon. Action oriented describes what it actually does and doesn't make people depressed as soon as they hear it. Wrangling is what you think it is—*wrastlin'* that there data into a place where we can control it! In case "wrastlin'" isn't a familiar term, it is like wrestling but involves more mud and muck. And that's exactly how data wrangling feels!

Before there is a highly refined data model, supporting architecture, and a corresponding process that helps folks who know
what to do with it all, we have to figure some things out. Data
wrangling is all about early-stage data preparation where we get
the data somewhere we can use it before we decide if it is worth
putting it somewhere more robust.

**Data wrangling involves identifying potential data use
cases, identifying source(s) of data to support them,
and mocking up prototypes to see if our hypotheses
have merit.**

This sounds a lot like data science, and that is because
data scientists often spend too much of their time wrangling.
Preparing data for use generally adds lower value than

performing fancy analyses, which is what data scientists should be spending most of their time doing. If we want to get the most out of our data science investments, we should teach the data to walk before the scientists make it dance later.

Wrangling is about taking relatively ambiguous ideas about potential data value and then doing a rough cut of what might eventually evolve into a production solution. This is a departure from how they did things in old-world data shops, where everything was predetermined before anybody had a chance to learn anything from the development process itself. One of my favorite ways to do some wrangling is by looking at the free data at the National Oceanic and Atmospheric Association (NOAA) website at https://noaa.gov. This is a treasure trove of weather data, and it is presented in many different groupings and formats.

Hailing from Chicago, I know too well the impact weather has on whether I want to leave the house. Seeing as it's often extremely cold or hot, sometimes in the same week, I keep a close eye on the forecast and current conditions. I also imagine that the businesses that depend on me leaving the house do the same. Wouldn't it be nice to create a simple model to determine how the temperature impacts sales? The sales data will be easy to find, even if it is something as simple as a log of daily cash deposits at the bank. Heading over to NOAA's website, we can find daily temperature data for the Chicago area. Download the files, open them with a data processing program like Excel, and go from there!

We may find that after working with the data a while, the insights are amazing, and we end up building much more sophisticated predictive models to anticipate based on future forecasting whether our business might need more or less inventory to handle the customer flow. Or maybe we find that it doesn't tell us anything valuable, and our business would be better off focusing on online sales or moving to San Diego, where it is pretty darn nice every day. This is a fine result too, because with data wrangling, we are exploring and trying out ideas without huge commitments. We won't know unless we try, and it is far better to try small first.

It used to be that data projects were always done using a waterfall project management methodology. This is when the entire plan is specified from the beginning, and the detailed work flows down from the higher-level objectives. Timelines are fairly rigid, and the amount of up-front specification is much higher than what we just described, where we jumped in and started figuring it out. Waterfall project management gives false comfort to the people paying for the project, because so many of the details are laid out from the beginning.

The problem is that so much of our knowledge and under-standing, and in turn optimal decision-making, is dependent on other things we know. Waterfall projects incorrectly imply that all relevant information is known during the design phase, but the truth is that we learn new things constantly throughout a project. Those new learnings should be applied to drive optimal designs and decisions for the rest of the project, and waterfall methodologies only accommodate in-flight changes through friction-heavy change requests and refactoring processes.

Waterfall data projects tend to flow like real waterfalls: smooth for a while, until the end when everything comes crashing down!

Wrangling is antithetical to waterfall project methodologies. Wrangling is a discovery process with a high degree of uncertainty and will propel learning and movement in ways that cannot be easily predicted. Sure, we could conceivably wrap all this in a waterfall project, but why would we if the project management methodology adds nothing to help the actual work succeed? Then it becomes overhead for the sake of overhead, and this is not something we data professionals should be advocating that we do.

That said, the tools of wrangling are as varied as data itself.

When I am working on new data sourcing, my preference is to read file specs, try to view in a text editor (if applicable and if the data file is small enough), or load it into a relational database. For very large files, data profiling tools that work at large scale can be helpful. Other data sources like streaming can require different tools and techniques. Python and microservices have enabled entirely new ways of processing data. Though the tools are incredibly varied, which one is best largely depends on our personal technical proclivities and the types of data we are looking at.

Once we select the technologies we want to work with, we need to (for lack of a better term) play with the data. See if the data reflects its specifications (typically documentation is low on developers' priority lists). Figure out how we might join it to our existing data and what path it might take to achieve the data value use cases we have in mind.

Wrangling is equal parts design and tinkering. It does not have a lot of prescribed activities, but it should result in a better understanding of what it will take to develop a more complete solution that will have a positive ROI. I like to think of wrangling as a loose collection of mini proofs of concept that will help us figure out the costs and benefits of options while minimizing the costs of doing that research.

....

Wrangling as a DLF discipline is like investing in research and development: spending some energy here will lead to improvements and efficiencies throughout everything else we do.

....

Wrangling, when done effectively, will have a strong value proposition in the risk management area. It does this by helping us explore in a smaller, cheaper context whether our ideas for larger scale efforts will lead to something valuable. Wrangling also contributes to revenue increases by identifying new opportunities and cost decreases by informing better development approaches to avoid unnecessary mistakes and rework. Many times, the techniques we prototype in the wrangling area eventually make it into the final projects.

I personally enjoy doing wrangling. It is an essential part of the design and architecture process. Just like a chef might want to touch and taste their ingredients or visit the place from which their ingredients came, data leaders will want to get close to the sources of data. Remember, many data sources are internally grown, so the above statement implies that data leaders will need to get close to the operations of their own organization. This means the systems, sure, but also the people and processes that are involved.

Later, we will try to influence these systems, people, and processes, but right now, we just want to understand them. Will we ever have credibility in suggesting that things be done differently if we have not fully learned how they are done now? If we do not understand how things are done, will we have a hope of identifying why they are being done this way? The answer to both of those questions is no. Sorry, rhetorical questions bother me.

Data wrangling in many ways is a more tactical instantiation of data leadership as a whole. Data leadership is not simply about achieving a Zen-like balance across data management topics. If we cast the light from each of the DLF disciplines at the problem, we will illuminate what we need to do to improve.

Data leadership is about going down the road less traveled. The sources of the data pain in our organizations are likely found in areas of the DLF where the least energy is being expended.

Fixing them all, on the other hand, is a bigger challenge. It is a start to know what each of the disciplines are, what they do to promote data value, and how they relate to one another, but as we've mentioned before, this just scratches the surface of any individual topic.

With data leadership in general and data wrangling in particular, the most important thing to do is start doing it. Be inquisitive, solve problems, and break through the walls ourselves. If we are starting out in the smallest or most inexperienced environment, a little data security, a little data wrangling, and a little bit of insight about what data might help change for the better—these alone might be enough to move the needle and get your data efforts going.

That is another important lesson: Do not expect to be good at it all or, especially in the early days, to even get to it all. In the world of data, we might have more blind spots than we do proficiencies, and that is okay. Only a fool would think they can handle all these on their own. What we need to do is be realistic about what we are working with and not extend past the breaking point. That said, we will absolutely need to push past the comfortable point. Data leadership is all about pushing ourselves and our organizations beyond where we are comfortable, because that is why we are behind in the first place!

To do that, we're going to need to build something. That's when development kicks in.

DEVELOPMENT

One of the most difficult things about working in a small business is that we never quite know where the breaking point is. We become so accustomed to wearing different hats that we think we can wear every hat, all the time. This is often because, though we sure would like to hire experts to do everything, resources are limited, and our spending priorities gravitate more toward electricity for the office and paying the salaries of the people we do have.

I once determined that the ETL tools that were available to me (for free) were subpar and that I could do better. I spent several months building my own ETL tool, using technologies I'd never used before, with very high expectations for myself. I pushed hard day and night and managed to create something objectively impressive in a short amount of time—with very limited assistance. It was one of the most frustrating yet invigorating periods in my career. I later got some help from a more practiced developer to smooth some of the rough edges, but it remained my design. It took a little doing, but we managed to get it in production for a client, and it is still running for them today.

Looking back on it, I'm not entirely sure whether this is an inspirational tale about following your ridiculous dreams to do something you probably shouldn't or whether this is a cautionary warning that these ideas are ridiculous, and you should perhaps be a little more careful with your ambition and time. Regardless, at some point in working with data, we are going to need to build something that does not yet exist.

This is development. The stakes are higher than for wrangling, as now we're actively building toward larger scale with commensurately higher investments and higher expectations. This is where data value is born! Through the data capabilities we build, we give our businesses the connection to data-driven improvement opportunities.

....

When we begin development, we should have already proven through wrangling that our data value use cases are achievable, and now we are building out the full capabilities with the goal of releasing them to production.

....

Think about the interplay here between development, wrangling, and architecture. Architecture informs the biggest brushstrokes, including the technologies we will use and the overall design integration. Wrangling proves out the smallest details, ensuring that we have the component pieces of data and process that we will ultimately need to have figured out. Development is where we really build our future.

Often, we start as a data development team of one, but most of the time, we will need help to build the capabilities we need. A starting development team of two or three is more common and more useful, as people tend to gravitate to different specialties. We can loosely break these roles down between front end (UI/UX), back end (integration), and database (modeling and performance).

Our front-end, UI/UX (user interface/user experience) folks enjoy building what people see and interact with. They have a knack for designing what is pleasant to the eyes. These teams can build websites and applications and are great at helping with building dashboards and interactive reporting solutions. They can often lend a hand with our marketing efforts, especially in the early days. Later, we can specialize further with developers and designers, but when starting out, we will be happy if we have anybody who loosely fits this role.

The back-end integration specialists are the salt of the earth. With tools like Java, Python, and C++ (for the hard core), these are the folks who unite the pretty things with the power of databases. They build out business logic through applications, connecting to APIs, and generally solving problems and making stuff work however they can. Back-end developers are likely to be the ones trumpeting the cloud, microservices architectures, and serverless infrastructure. They also tend to champion open-source software, laptop stickers, and free T-shirts. If you can only bring one developer to your efforts, it probably needs to be somebody who identifies as part of this back-end integration specialist group but can fake it till they make it on front-end and database work.

Finally, database specialists are the heavy machinery operators of the bunch. Good ones have expanded their horizons to move beyond the monolithic relational databases and see the value in new technologies, helping to bridge the knowledge gap between traditional data storage and warehousing and back-end application developers. Old-school database people are implanted with microchips that cause them to deny the existence of new database technologies like graph, NoSQL, and blockchain. Regardless, database folks must build out the systems that house billions of data records, serving up information to a myriad of system and human endpoints. It takes a unique set of skills and compulsion to be great at this stuff.

Development is a big topic by itself, just like the DLF disciplines. Don't be afraid to start, but do be afraid to try to do it all on your own.

Things only get more complex from here. We can have entire teams dedicated to each of these functions. In fact, larger organizations will have entire teams dedicated to *parts* of these functions. We haven't even talked about things like deployment, DevOps (and its younger sibling DataOps), and all the fancy data orchestration techniques we can use. The rabbit hole of technologies and clever names is endless, so we are certainly not going to do them justice here. Just remember that data value is what matters most, and all the technologies and other complications are details on the data leadership journey.

As you might imagine, coordinating efforts among all these development folks can take some serious energy of its own. Fortunately, there's a DLF discipline for that! Admittedly, that is not quite as catchy as "there's an app for that!"—but we also don't have Apple's marketing budget. In fact, we should be happy that we have a catchphrase at all. Most data books don't even have that!

So much of the rest of the DLF is about the business implications of data, whether it's improving its usefulness or being used and eventually driving the differentials in business outcomes. The entire DLF access category skews technical because this is where the foundation is laid. To build great capabilities through the rest of the DLF, we must have sound technology fundamentals from which to support our lofty business-facing ambition.

Data access is where it all begins. Where we can start working with data before we even know whether it will be of any value in the end. Where we can experiment at low risk and low costs, finding the best ideas from which to develop lasting solutions. Where data technologists can play with data from their home in the dark catacombs of our office buildings, where they won't scare the pretty people.

It's data access that is the doorway to the rest of the data capabilities we will build. Once the data is in-house, we can accomplish anything! And we will. In the next chapter, we look at the ways we turn data from the raw materials into the insights that will transform our organizations! Are we excited yet? Let's do this!

CITATION

1 Alex Schiffer, "How a Fish Tank Helped Hack a Casino," *Washington Post*, July 21, 2017, https://www.washingtonpost.com/news/innovations/wp/2017/07/21/how-a-fish-tank-helped-hack-a-casino/?noredirect=on.

8

REFINE: BUILD POTENTIAL

BRIDGE THE GAP BETWEEN RAW DATA AND USEFUL INFORMATION

Refinement is where we focus on assessing and strategically improving our data so it fulfills the business impacts we have in mind. We must process and make data suitable for many uses, just like crude oil is refined into gasoline, kerosene, plastics, and candy corn. That last one might be made up, but if there were a candy that came from processing crude oil, it would have to be candy corn.

To maximize data value, we know we will drive changes in human behavior by using data. It only makes sense that we also need to change the data a bit too. Since data is the output of processes that exist to do something beyond simply creating data, we should expect that data isn't precisely what we need the moment we establish access to it.

If we want to change human behavior with data, we should optimize data to make it easier.

We have limited opportunities to change how the data is formed when it first reaches us. Most of the time, we must work with what we get, just like oil refiners have to deal with variances in chemicals due to different climate and dead dinosaur factors that created the crude oil. Though it might be fun to call the data coming from sources *crude* data, we're sure somebody would get upset about it. Nevertheless, our ability to create data-driven changes in business outcomes depends on this DLF category.

CONTEXT

In earlier versions of the DLF, I called this section "metadata." Everybody hates that word, and because of this, I'm afraid people were inclined to skip right past this section and go straight to data quality. This is what the data gangs call "a suboptimal ontological methodology." These are data gangs, after all—their slang ain't the hippest.

This reminds me of a time in elementary school when my class played a word game where you had to quickly make as many words as you can from the letters in another word. I never won this game, except once I did. The word was LANGUAGES, and I thought it would be awesome if "SLANGUAGE" was also a word, so I put it down knowing there was no downside beyond my own pride when it was challenged. And sure enough, it did get challenged, and it was a word! I got some crazy triple-word-score bonus and crushed the competition that day. Never even came close to winning that word game again, but for that one day, I was a legend!

··

A willingness to be ridiculously wrong may be the path to unexpected success.

··

Data context is not just about the boring obvious stuff like what database the data is in or that Jane is the owner. Context is a story of data that tells us what the data is really all about and informs us how we can use the data.

And...spoiler alert...this is what data quality is all about! In the next section when we get to data quality, we'll focus on the fitness of the data for use, which means the context of data is everything not covered by data quality! Let's investigate further, and since we're serious about this, we'll stick to the formal terms and stop making up better words (like "slanguage").

If we want to use data to create positive change, first we need to know where things stand now. This is fundamentally what metadata management is about. Data nerds who like being clever over being helpful define metadata as "data about data." While this is technically true, people tend to ignore this definition as silly talk that makes no sense. This is also technically true, as recursive logic is often difficult for our human brains to understand.

Attempting to be both helpful and handsome, I prefer to define metadata as "anything that provides context to data." Metadata tells the story of data, and that story can often be more useful than the data itself. Here's why.

4

That number four up there is data. Do you recall how I told you at the very beginning of this book that data is lazy? Not very useful sitting around by itself, is it?

What if I told you that the lazy number up there represents how many cookies each child will receive?

What if I told you that it was the number of days since we last had a fatal workplace accident?

What if I told you it is just a number I chose to explain metadata and then had to make up some other examples?

The context of the data matters. A lot. Perhaps your reaction when we were talking about cookies was "Heck, yeah! Cookie time!" Or it could have been "Hmm. Four cookies seems like a lot for a child. Should we really be advocating contributing to the childhood obesity epidemic?" The workplace accident example probably raised your level of attentiveness and caused a dozen additional questions to flood your mind. The final explanation, though actually correct in this example, seems like a waste of a good number four.

This exercise teaches us that a number four is not terribly interesting by itself. But hopefully it also illustrates that metadata is pretty much everything we think about when we think we are thinking about data. Yes, that is a lot of *thinking*, and that's why most people would prefer to ignore metadata entirely, but now we know better!

It's as if data is the earth, and the metadata is the earth's atmosphere. We must have the earth to stand on, but without air, we're never going to get to those cookies we are clearly obsessed with.

Metadata describes the world around us. It provides a more complete understanding of our businesses today so we can improve our businesses tomorrow.

Metadata comes in two basic flavors: technical and business. Technical metadata is by far the most common since every technology system creates metadata of some sort. These can take the form of log files, databases, configuration settings, system reports—you name it. Technical metadata is easy to access (pun intended!) and put somewhere where it can be used for data value purposes.

The downside of technical metadata is that it is so abundant that it has lots of worthless stuff in with the good, creating a low–data value density.

Yes, I do think we coined that term just now! Pretty exciting, eh? "Data value density" is a measure of data value per unit of data. It is the benefit we are likely to create down the road if we go through the trouble of capturing and analyzing a batch of data compared with a batch of any other data. The goal is to find relatively low-effort ways to compile data with high–data value density (like internal order data) before taking on high-effort activities that have low data value density (like the Twitter firehose, which is a feed of all the tweets). In its simplest terms, let's first do the easy stuff that will drive the biggest benefits.

Data value density is an especially important consideration when we think about big data (again, like the Twitter firehose), which is when there is so much volume and complexity in the data that it becomes unwieldy to work with. The data value density concept applies in a lot of settings, including here with metadata. Technical metadata is a low–data value density asset that takes relatively little effort to compile—not the worst thing to spend a little time on, but we should temper expectations of what it will do for us.

In contrast, business metadata has a high–data value density. This is because, by definition, it has business relevance. This is metadata that comes from people's brains. It can be conveyed through documentation, conversations, the Excel spreadsheets Barb puts together—you name it. Business metadata is so valuable because it cannot be created without people making a dedicated effort, and if that effort isn't made, the knowledge could be lost forever.

Let's consider one of the favorite activities of a data governance organization: compiling agreed-on definitions of business terms into a business glossary. This is first and foremost a metadata management exercise. We are reaching into the business to identify business metadata, with a corresponding (meta)data quality initiative to consolidate varied interpretations into coherent definitions that reflect the best available understanding of truth.

Another extension of metadata is data lineage. Data lineage is metadata over time: it tells the life story of data as it is created, refined, aggregated, and used as part of a data value proposition. Data lineage can be a powerful tool to understand how a piece of information made it to a report we are viewing and why two numbers that seem like they should match don't.

One risk we can stumble into when taking on a metadata-driven exercise is to jump too quickly into looking for solutions. For example, if we ask Jim to give us a definition of a customer, we might be tempted to lead him by telling him Sally's definition. Jim will be inclined to anchor his response based on Sally's and maybe even just agree entirely. We could have extracted some meaningful insights from variances in definitions, but instead we took a shortcut and missed an opportunity to do a better job. This happens all the time, and people usually have no idea they are making mistakes.

Data leaders should advocate judgment-free metadata management. Do not impose what your view of truth should be; simply capture what is there, for better or worse.

We will have plenty of time to get judgy and try to change the world later, but if we are working from a faulty map, it will hurt those efforts down the road. The resources to teach us good judgment-free metadata management techniques may appear to be lacking, at least if we plug that specific term into a search box.

There are plenty of tools that help us collect business metadata and countless ways to compile technical metadata. But to get started, we should pick our favorite spreadsheet program and track down interesting metadata stories. By the time we hate our spreadsheet program, we will know what we need from a more capable tool.

Just be warned, if we start with powerful tools before we've outgrown what we already have, we will not only waste money but miss out on important context. Tool shortcuts can be just as dangerous as process mistakes! We should earn the tools we buy. Don't buy something because we might run into a wall without it. Wait until we can see the wall with enough clarity to realize that to get past it, we're going to need a bigger hammer.

So many resources are wasted on tools that are underuti-lized. Metadata repository, data catalog, data dictionary, data lineage—these are all important context functions that we will need to consider. But getting somebody to swing a mediocre hammer is still going to accomplish more than even the greatest Thor hammer sitting on a table with nobody picking it up.

Focus energy on motivating people first and optimizing tools second. This helps us achieve more efficiency in our resource investments and provides a valuable secondary benefit: we can learn and calibrate our activities in a smaller, safer context before we amplify them with more powerful tools. Since optics are important, we want to limit the blast radius of our mistakes while amplifying when we get it right.

Just like with a stereo speaker, any amplifier makes unwanted noise louder too. That is, unless we can remove that noise. Hello, data quality!

QUALITY

In contrast to "metadata management," which is a complex term to describe relatively simple concepts, "data quality" is a seemingly simple term that confuses everybody. Because the words "data" and "quality" are familiar, people logically infer that we are talking about making data as good (i.e., high quality) as it can be. This is an incomplete and oversimplified understanding of what is a much more diverse subject.

In practice, this flawed notion of data quality has caused rampant data trust issues, because we have essentially set expectations that data needs to be perfect to be worth using. Not true! In absence of anything else, we certainly prefer higher-quality data to lower-quality data, but if our goal is to create maximum data value compared to the resources and energy expended, we need a better understanding of what data quality really is.

Data quality is a discipline to assess and optimize data's suitability for use in data value-creating endeavors.

Let's break this down a little bit more:

- **Data quality is a discipline that we see everywhere in data management. Even if we disagree on the specifics of the definition, we can agree that data quality is important.**
- **Assessing and optimizing data's suitability for use is the heart of it all. Data quality is first about understanding the specific aspects of data that make it useful or not useful. This**

is an extension of metadata management, where we are now applying judgment to figure out whether the truth that exists is optimal for the actual demands we will place on the data to drive data value activities. Where it is suboptimal, we may strategically choose to apply additional energy to the data to improve its usefulness. Public works projects are a great example of this, where the data says a pipe to be replaced is twelve inches, but the data is also seventy-five years old. This is the kind of situation where a little data quality improvement up front can save a lot of leaking pipes later.

- Data value-creating endeavors imply that data will often have more than one use. We need to look at as many of them as we can and factor the collective needs into our prioritization. Data isn't just created for one purpose, even though data consumers are often only interested in one of those purposes at any time. Thinking about patterns and the overall system is important as we evaluate even singular data quality items.

And this is why understanding this data quality definition is so important. When we take the time to understand which data will drive value, how much value we estimate that to be, and what the suitability characteristics of that data are, only then can we prioritize our data quality efforts!

The alternative is haphazardly applying resources allocated to data quality in the hopeless pursuit of perfection, typically in response to whoever is complaining loudest. So how does this work?

We must first figure out where the data in question falls on this data quality suitability-for-use spectrum and apply a scoring methodology that will be meaningful to those who will use it. The best approach is to start simple to articulate basic usefulness and then iterate through the more complex aspects that determine suitability for our organization's needs. Then we will communicate these characteristics of the data to the folks who need it.

....

If we want data quality to matter in our organizations, a *suitability-for-use* assessment should accompany any data used to drive business outcomes.

....

Suitability-for-use assessments evaluate and document what we know about the usefulness of the data based on metadata and any contextual clues we can find. We should try to be as objective as possible in compiling these, as we don't necessarily know all the potential uses for the data we are evaluating. Even if we're compiling the suitability-for-use assessment with a particular use case in mind, we want future users of the data to be able to evaluate their situations as easily as possible.

....

Never share data without a quality understanding.[*]

....

---

[*] Yes, I intended both ways you can read this, and I thought I was *mighty* clever in doing so. If you find more than two, I didn't intend those...*unless* they are even better, in which case I *definitely* intended those too. Why are you still down here reading jokes? There are some great points up there. Get back to work!

Now, here comes an unfortunate truth. When is the last time we saw a suitability-for-use assessment accompanying data in a report or application? "Never" is sadly the most likely answer. A suitability-for-use assessment, often distilled into a data quality score, can be as thorough or simple as the situation warrants. Like so many of the data leadership topics we discuss, knowing the concept exists and that some attention needs to be given to it is far more important than the specifics of how we do it.

It could start as simple as a spreadsheet that lists the following:

- **Date of assessment**
- **Data source**
- **Data attribute**
- **Intended use**
- **Suitability evaluation**
- **Assessor name**

Maybe it starts as a reference document published as part of your data service offerings. Down the road, you could add these findings to a tool that provides integrated insights so that data consumers have this information alongside the data itself.

Everything with data quality outlined above should seem obvious, yet very few organizations seem to have figured this out. If we agree that data needs to be suitable for its intended use, then without any guidance on what that suitability is, what will rational people do? They will assume the data is perfect, and when it turns out not to be perfect, they stop trusting the data. They will then blame the data people who provided the information, because who else are they going to blame? We are the ones who are supposed to make sure the data is right! And they were never told that the data might be unsuitable for their use.

If we continue letting people make blind assumptions about data's suitability for use, we will never improve data quality, and we will struggle to create data value.

If nothing else, we must educate folks that imperfect data *can* be trusted. After all, *all* data is imperfect in some way. Maybe the sensors that captured the temperature were plus or minus one degree. Maybe a customer entered their address online and accidentally typed the wrong number. Even data that got captured "correctly" could have been delivered faster or had more context provided. There are always more things we can do with data, but that doesn't mean we should.

Just as important as getting folks comfortable with imperfection with data, we also have to inform them when we know data is unsuitable for the uses they intend. We can work with people to allocate resources and prioritization to help the data reach the usefulness they need, but without more transparency in our interactions, this misunderstanding of data quality will only get worse.

So now that we understand data's suitability for use, we can probably think of examples where the data in our companies currently isn't good enough to use for what people want. This gives us an opportunity to implement a data quality improvement initiative that has measurable objectives. We can say things like, "Our data is currently a 75 overall data quality score, but for the intended use, we need 85, so we must devote resources to improve the completeness and verified subscores by 20 percent. This will require approximately sixty hours of effort at X dollars per hour."

At the same time, we can tie the intended use to a data value creation estimate and then compare the costs to expected benefits to inform the prioritization of what we are going to do! Using the data value principles we've discussed, we now have a quantification of our data quality improvement opportunities! We can do this kind of exercise for any of the DLF disciplines and then compare where we'll likely get our best ROI.

But improving suboptimal data quality is only one option. If we are really concerned with maximizing ROI (or data value), we should evaluate the potential sources of data quality issues and take action to prevent those problems from creating data that will cause problems downstream. Cleaning up data is almost always a painful and costly exercise—best to avoid it entirely whenever possible. As in health, prevention is the best medicine!

....

The most efficient way to improve data quality is to prevent issues from occurring when the data is created.

....

Data is born when something is measured and recorded. Errors are more likely to occur here than any other place, and the further away from this moment an error is discovered, the more costly and difficult (or impossible) improving the data quality will be. Data creation is the first step of the data life cycle, which is how data goes from being created to moving through systems and business processes to ultimately being put in its final resting place. Data's final resting place is usually either some sort of cold storage solution where the data isn't easy to access but could be accessed if it is needed for an unanticipated reason or nowhere, as in deleted.

Deleting data is often overkill and other times mandatory. It depends on a variety of factors, including internal policies or laws that require it. The GDPR in Europe mandates the right to be forgotten, meaning that a person can request their data be deleted. If not honored, companies could be fined millions of euros for noncompliance. Data life cycle is a big deal, and you'd better believe data quality is a big part of it!

While data quality issues can creep in at any point in the data life cycle, the system that initially records the information is the single biggest contributor to data quality. Solving for speed and precision at data creation makes dealing with any downstream issues much easier. But what if we are further downstream, dealing with data created by entirely different areas of our organization or even another organization entirely?

It still doesn't hurt to try to get improvements at the source, but we may find our efforts futile. In this case, we need to triage as far upstream as possible or simply recognize that attempting to remediate some data will not be worth the effort. We never have enough resources to do everything we would like to do.

By quantifying value, we can optimally allocate scarce resources across any data initiatives we are considering, regardless of whether they are data quality, data governance, systems related, etc. For true data quality aficionados, this quantified data quality approach should raise an eyebrow when extended to its logical limit. Though the common misconception (thoroughly debunked above, if I do say so myself) indicates a "perfection or nothing" default approach, the truth is that aiming for perfect data quality is always a mistake. "Good enough to use everywhere" is a much better target.

This is where master data management and its nearly identical twin reference data management come into the data quality picture. These functions collect and coordinate usage of the most frequently used data sets in our organizations. Definitions of regions, product categories, customer classifications, states, and zip codes—these are a few examples.

> **When master data is managed well, systems are easier to keep aligned, and data can flow more freely. One might think of these as data quality amplifiers. We would.**

When the same data is used in multiple places but not managed holistically as one data set, these data sets will inevitably diverge over time. People may have the best intentions, but without coordination, even well-intended changes will cause differences. Then as the data is used throughout the respective systems, the uniqueness becomes more ingrained.

Reconciling incongruent master data sets is a special kind of pain. Think of a fast-growing company that has regional salespeople who earn commissions on what is sold in their areas. Over time, the company hires more people and modifies the sales territories, but the system that tracks the actual sales is drawing its information from an outdated map. People manage their behavior based on how sales reports indicate they are doing. What happens if a technologist finds the error and fixes it without warning?

Chaos!

The salespeople think all their numbers are wrong. Executives are mad because things are not lining up to their expectations. Data quality has arguably improved, but people are up in arms. Worse, since people have been operating on faulty information, they have inadvertently been generating commissions for other reps, and now management has lost the ability even to know which salespeople are the most productive.

This is the impact from one master data set that was updated somewhat slowly. Imagine the risk across most organizations that have no master data proficiency at all! How many data sets that should be the same in practice have different versions?

Managing customer accounts as master data is a bit of a holy grail for master data programs. Some might argue that customer data can be too voluminous to truly be considered master data. My counterpoint is that if we mess up customer data, what do we plan to get right instead? Customer data is as important as it gets.

Customer data will need to be referenced by systems throughout the data life cycle. Keeping it consistent is a high priority. Many organizations are challenged to define who their customers even are, let alone maintain data consistency throughout all the systems that reference customers. From a strategic point of view, for organizations earlier on the data maturity curve, master data should be considered enough to avoid making things unnecessarily difficult for our future selves.

For example, if we are building out a new data mart, it would likely be a good use of energy to see if we can reuse existing customer sets, or even better, establish a lasting precedent for merging multiple customer sets into a consolidated customer master that can be extended throughout the organization. It may feel arduous or like scope creep in the moment, but this kind of surgical strike with master data has the potential to save thousands of dollars (or more!) down the road. This is the risk management side of data value in full effect!

At the limit, diminishing marginal returns in the pursuit of perfection will consume infinite resources while driving zero meaningful difference in business outcomes. Executives often make decisions with 70 percent or less confidence levels, as they cannot delay decisions until more complete information is available. Rocket scientists and pharmacists, by comparison, often require higher levels of confidence before moving forward.

When there is a sufficiently high likelihood of the optimal result, stop trying to make the data better! There are other data quality problems that need solving.

Why keep trying to improve data that already drives the best possible business outcomes? Once the right decision or activity is likely, we must divert precious data quality improvement resources to data assets that need the help more.

But data rightfully now has people's attention, and we must start putting in better data quality practices that will help all our organizations reach their potential. To correct the perception of data quality, we must have the courage to address these items head-on and ensure that we make the most of any resources that come our way. With data quality scoring, suitability-for-use assessments, and issue prevention actions, we will truly help our organizations get better at what they do.

Being excellent at data quality provides an outstanding foundation for data leadership capabilities in every discipline. Getting going with data quality is probably an important data refinement discipline for all organizations, and the next three refinement disciplines build on an assumption that data quality is sufficiently optimized. As we compare it to the other DLF disciplines, data quality may not be the absolute highest priority on our list, but it should be close to the top.

ENRICHMENT

Data quality helps us assess the data we have and, among other things, identify where the data is insufficient to meet our business needs. Sometimes we can fix things on our own, but other times, we need to go outside our walls for added help.

Data enrichment is supplementing our internally available data sources with external resources. It is additive and will supply context to data that you already have (underneath it is metadata, just like pretty much everything!).

As with all things data, we need to be judicious in how we obtain external resources. Some will be provided for a cost, while other data sources will be free. You may get weather data for analysis from NOAA, as mentioned earlier or pay for contact information lists to drive your sales efforts. Be a bit wary of free data, especially if not coming from public/open data sources. Under the best circumstances, free data sources may be not easy to use, infrequently updated, or formatted in an arcane method. In the worst circumstances, the data may be incomplete, inaccurate, or unauthorized, and by using it, we may face serious legal consequences.

Enrichment resources available for a fee tend to follow the "you get what you pay for" rule. Dun & Bradstreet, for example, has amassed a staggering amount of highly curated information about businesses of all kinds. They include basic location data but also industry classifications, employee and revenue numbers, names and contact information of leaders, and seemingly anything else they can get their hands on! They know their information is prized, so they charge a premium for it. Deciding whether it is an attractive ROI is going to be a different exercise for every organization.

We keep bringing up the NOAA website. They provide a rich resource of weather information gathered from weather stations throughout the world. This information is great for establishing weather-based analysis to identify patterns in customer behavior, employee absenteeism, and other product performance metrics. And it's free! Use it for wrangling, use it for enrichment, use it for...um, that's it, I think. But that's still a couple of really important things!

Every organization should be looking at weather information to help assess past performance and predict future behaviors. If we could do something as simple as avoiding under- and overstaffing situations, what would the outcome be worth? A lot! Restaurants often have busy and slow periods that correlate with the weather, but how many are proactively staffing based on the weather predictions? Not enough!

This is an exciting one-step-removed-from-actual-value kind of data analysis—you bet that's the kind of impact we want to make! From there, we can build on our rudimentary weather analysis and find supplementary data to build models that help us understand the influence of everything from holidays to conventions to what the impact is when the VFW hall next door hosts a fish fry.

And that last one is important! Not only do we love the idea of old-school fish fries, but we don't need to work for a large organization to make this worthwhile. Any individual reading this book has the mental fortitude to learn how to acquire data, put it into a place where they can work with it, and then do some analysis that will help their business.

Even if we are looking at daily cash deposit amounts from a bank statement against daily high temps in our area from NOAA, it may tell us a story that helps us do something different to make our business better. Will every data enrichment opportunity be hugely beneficial? Nope. Not even close. But it is still worth it, because those that work out will exceed the cost of effort from all of them.

....

While it is very *human* to want simple answers, it's not very *data*.

....

Data enrichment is a counterpoint to the silly notion of a single source of truth. Consider this analogy: if you have a statue on a pedestal in a museum, how can you illuminate it to provide the best viewing experience for the guest? Is it by shining a flashlight on it? No, that leads to a shadow-puppet nightmare. It is best to cast light from several different directions, blanketing the statue in a balanced glow.

It's the same for illuminating truth with data. We need many points of perspective, provided by different sources of data, given appropriate data context and usability insights from data quality and related functions. We can't know ahead of time the specific context a data consumer will be using to see a particular truth, so the best approach is to provide a balanced glow that is as accurate as possible from any direction. Data enrichment can be thought of as the fine-tuning necessary to get the balance just right.

Like I mentioned earlier, doing a lot of data enrichment is of minimal value before our metadata and data quality capabilities are in good shape. But once core capabilities have been established, data enrichment can become a valuable addition to our data value story. As we go down the path of adding more to our data, we run the risk of creating so much that people lose sight of what is most worthwhile, or we inadvertently spend too much energy maintaining data sources and outputs that are not worth the effort.

CURATION

There is a lot going on in this DLF category! From the other disciplines we've discussed, we already have an impressive amount of potential value that we can create. With increasing potential value comes complexity, and complexity begets additional costs, and we do not like creating costs. Therefore, curation is the final discipline within the data refinement category. We need to be deliberate about the data and capabilities in which we continue to invest and those that are better off deprecated.

....

Data curation is the art of removing the unnecessary.

....

When we think of curation, we tend to think of what is included, like in a museum gallery, because the exhibit is defined by what we see. But look around—*everything* is oriented toward what is included. Curation is really about removing anything unessential so that the important stuff shines through. This is not a standard definition of curation but is intended to highlight what is important but often overlooked.

Think of our objective as cultivating data bonsai trees. Just like we must focus our energy to create a balanced system of DLF categories, we can further boost efficiency by actively removing unnecessary waste from the system.

Though we might think this is all implied as part of other DLF disciplines, in practice, it is largely overlooked. People are wired to come up with new ideas and pursue them. We like to have brainstorming sessions where we think of anything and everything that might expand our capabilities. Anyone who has ever been in a brainstorming session knows that most of the ideas are embarrassingly terrible, but a few special ideas have enough potential to be worth taking further action on. These justify the meeting because we see the opportunity to add value by acting. This mentality aligns to the *increasing revenue* part of the data value equation.

Just as "a dollar saved is as good as a dollar earned," we should spend as much effort assessing the value of shutting down underperforming activities as we spend brainstorming new ones. Why don't we ever have "antibrainstorming" meetings where we actively abandon current activities not living up to their potential? These meetings would likely be more effective than brainstorming meetings because we will have more data available to drive our conclusions! In any setting, we are going to have a lot of valuable ideas and even more that aren't worth it. It's the rough that comes along with the diamond. To get to the good stuff, we must experiment, but we don't have to continue investing in the bad ideas once we know they are bad.

....

The worst thing we can do is never make a mistake.

....

As we know by now, data is an imperfect art. We can have all the data we want, refined and as suitable for use as it can be, analyzed with the best tools and techniques available, and we are still capable of making the wrong decision. This is because the future can't be predicted completely.

This implies that if we wait to act until we are nearly certain that we won't be wrong, we will have missed out on most of the possible value! Effecting business change, the source of data value, necessarily comes with some amount of risk. We normally think of this as a motivator to get moving, but what happens when we try to run in every direction at once? We get nowhere. We also probably look foolish flailing around like that.

If we use our moments of wrongness to learn and change

our future behaviors, then next time, we will be a little bit more likely to get it right. In poker, they say never chase bad money with good money—that means once we see we misjudged a situation and will lose the hand no matter what, we must stop putting money into it, fold our cards, and find another opportunity.

Back in the data world, these same lessons apply. If we build data analysis tools that people don't use, we need to recalibrate the tools, provide more training, or get the right data into them. Data curation is about observing the world around us, identifying the mistakes, and correcting our course of action. Throw that project plan away if it is not leading us down the right path.

Having the courage to lead means having the courage to be wrong.

Data curation is too often overlooked by organizations focused on building new things. In fact, even most data management texts and frameworks make no mention of it. This makes balancing the scales a function of always adding more, and at some point, the scales just cannot handle the weight. Whether that manifests in losing funding, getting fired, or simply being relegated as unimportant, this will be our fate if we continue to ignore data curation.

This entire data refinement category boils down to judiciously applying the resources we must to transform data to drive maximum business change. The first two DLF categories have focused more inwardly on what we can build and directly do with the data, creating maximum *potential* data value. The rest of the DLF focuses more outwardly on connecting the data to changing our businesses, and this is where the *real* data value arrives!

9

USE: DELIVER INSIGHTS

UNUSED DATA NEVER REALIZES ITS POTENTIAL
The third DLF category is all about connecting people to the data we made useful during the first two DLF categories. We may have built up considerable potential value in those activities, but that potential value will not become realized without people putting it to use. That's in fact why we call it "use"—if we want to create data value, we need to do something with this data. Later we'll figure out if the use was productive toward our goals, but first we need to learn the basics of how data does stuff.

> **Since creating data value depends on organizational change, once we have data worth using, we should focus the most effort toward connecting data to change catalysts.**

People can use data in countless ways, and the DLF disciplines that we outline in this category are intended to be representative but not necessarily comprehensive. And just like with data quality, we should not keep focusing our energies on making data better if we are struggling to realize the value that is already there.

The right way to do this is to get our businesses to leverage the basic insights first, like we talked about with the weather analysis in the enrichment section. Then we can learn from how the data drives positive change, and we can use that knowledge to improve what we do with the data going forward. Hey! How did the simple virtuous cycle sneak back in here? Because it's everywhere!

As we get into the details of the use DLF category, remember that these too are guides to help us think through our data-related challenges and opportunities from all directions. These are not prescriptive solutions on which to take a check-the-box mentality. It's probably clear by now that around these parts, we aren't too fond of check-the-box mentalities under most circumstances. It is something we need to do from time to time, but it's very rarely the right way to arrive at the best solution.

MODELING

Data models and the data repositories they represent are the traditional core of organizational data capabilities. These are our classic enterprise data environments, built around a data warehouse and responsible for a large part of the data value created in today's organizations. Many of the reports, dashboards, and visualizations that we build couldn't be created or maintained as effectively without a data warehouse or database sitting underneath them.

Modeling is how we take our understanding of truth and put the data that describes it into a form that both accurately reflects and efficiently delivers the information to those who wish to use it. *Data modeling* is how raw data gets structure, most commonly in databases, and for analytics purposes at scale, often in data warehouses.

Data warehouses were all the rage a decade or two ago, and for good reason. Data warehouses are good at a lot of things. If we want to serve up information to a variety of changing data consumption mechanisms for operational purposes, data warehouses have us covered. They provide consistency and performance to data consumers but require substantial effort to build.

Data modeling is considered with data warehousing because we cannot accomplish much data work without models, and models don't accomplish much without being instantiated through some sort of data repository. For data analytics purposes, this repository is most commonly a data warehouse database. Though this symbiotic (or codependent) relationship is real, it should in no way diminish the depth and importance of either data modeling or data warehousing.

People can have entire careers as data modelers, and some of the greatest thought leaders in the data management space are primarily data modelers at heart. Similarly, data warehousing professionals often have deep, specialized skill sets that combine technical proficiency in relational databases with the ability to design and shepherd the data that flows through them.

In a lot of ways, data modelers are the business side of the data architecture coin. Modelers create the conceptual and logical designs for data containment and hand them off to the physical designs led by data warehousing folks.

We might think of data modeling as designing how actual truth (real life) becomes approximated truth (data).

We have talked a little bit about data modeling and warehousing, but we have not yet addressed one key question about this DLF discipline. Are you thinking of it? The most obvious question is "What the heck is modeling doing in the use category?"

This, at first, seems to be a good question. The specific functions performed in modeling are certainly like those that we find throughout the access and refine categories. We're obviously working with the data, building conceptual structures, and creating systems and platforms to do things.

The big perspective shift represented in the modeling discipline is that we're now focused on the consumption of the data.

Ten or twenty years ago, we almost always modeled data before performing the bulk of data movement and transformation activities. That is, when we take source data that comes from various internal and external systems, it typically comes in a format specific to the source's needs, so we would transform it and bring it into our system in a format that works better for our needs. This is known as schema-on-write.

Schema-on-write means when data is moved into a new system, the data is put into a structured format as soon as it arrives in the new system.

A schema-on-write structure makes it easier for people and systems to use data effectively whenever they want. The downside is it takes time and effort to put everything into a structure up front, and if the data isn't used enough, all those efforts are wasted.

You may also encounter the term "extract-transform-load" (ETL) as part of the data life cycle:

- *Extract*: pull data out of a source system.
- *Transform:* change the data into a form better suited to our needs.
- *Load:* put the data into the new system.

It is worth noting that sometimes the order changes, such as ELT. This extract-load-transform accomplishes the same thing, but instead of changing the data as it moves between systems, we load it into the new system, then evolve it to be what we need it to be. It's a nuanced difference that we're noting here to save a future conversation when you might talk with a data architect, ask the question, and then must listen to them sigh loudly as if it is the most obvious thing in the world. It really isn't that obvious, so don't feel bad.

Also, this ELT pattern is more common now, as we typically move data as is into a data lake, which is the primary data repository. At most, we see some basic data normalization and refinements to get consistent file formats in the data lake, but that's about it. Since at the time we populate a data lake, we may have a limited view on how the data will eventually be used, we also have a limited perspective on how we might structure it. By leaving it unchanged as we put it into the data lake (also known as a "storage layer"), we save structuring the data for later, when the data is used. This is known as schema-on-read

....

In schema-on-read architectures, data is stored as it comes (in its "native" format). It's only when the data is used (i.e., "read") that a new structure is applied.

....

Schema-on-read has some advantages, like ensuring only data needed for use consumes structure-creating resources and that once data is written into the new system, it is always ready to be used. Downsides may include a lack of consistent structures for different uses that would ideally be identical. It may also be hard to figure out the appropriate structures for data, which could then delay the ability to use the data quickly.

While detailed data architecture recommendations are beyond our scope in this book, a good rule of thumb is the more frequently data is used and the more consistency required in that use, the more likely a schema-on-write design is preferable. Think about the classic data warehouse uses: financial reporting, sales patterns, and other operational metrics. For more exploratory uses like deep data science analysis or if the data may never be used at all, a schema-on-read design is likely the better option. For data scientists especially, it is often preferable to use data that hasn't gone through modeling, as the consistency modeling imparts also reduces noise and the fidelity of the original source.

Like how some people love the warm and crackly sound of an old-school record player, source data may be better for some purposes with the crackles removed, but for other purposes, the crackles are the precise outliers the user needs. Data use–level modeling lets us have it either way, whereas if modeling were oriented toward the refine or access categories, it would have the potential of removing exactly what some users want most. Not a data value–adding scenario, is it?

No. I still can't seem to get the hang of these rhetorical questions.

....

In almost any organization, there are "poison" terms that cause strong negative reactions whenever they are said. Pro tip: don't say those terms. Find something else to call them.

....

It seems like a rite of passage that organizations have one or two colossal data warehouse failures before they finally get it right. It's these big failures that lead to our colleagues having extra entrenched resistance to the idea of supporting data-driven change initiatives. *Data warehouse* and *data governance* are up there in the don't-say-that-around-here hall of fame. But just because these things were likely unsuccessful before your organization really understood data leadership doesn't mean that you shouldn't try again now that data value is even more important now than it was then.

Regardless of the names we choose to call these things, the importance of data modeling is not to be overlooked. Even though technology has become amazingly powerful, we must not fall into the trap of thinking that this is a function we no longer need. An in-memory visualization tool, for example, is not an adequate replacement for a properly modeled data layer. Even artificial intelligence is incapable (so far) of replacing a human's unique ability to model a database to fit an organization's specific data needs.

Data repositories themselves have exploded with options. Instead of always going into a data warehouse or other warm, always-on database, data used less frequently can be left in file-based object storage (like Amazon's S3). Technology even allows us to directly query those object stores like a database but without needing to perform any other file movements. The future is now!

....

Think of these cutting-edge technologies as complements to traditional data repositories, not replacements for them.

....

With all the improvements in technology, the right mix of capabilities for a single firm is going to be different from that of any other. The complexity of effective modeling increases as the variety of technology options grows. And like so many of the other disciplines we cover, we see overlap between this and other areas like data architecture and enterprise architecture.

This evolution is likely to continue at an ever-increasing rate. Though this domain of thought is not likely to go anywhere anytime soon, the longer it has been since this book was published, the more the specifics will continue to shift. If nothing else, working in the data space will always keep us on our toes!

REPORTING

Data repositories do not do much just sitting there by themselves. We need to get information out of them, and the simplest way to do that is through reports. Reporting is a unidirectional flow of information out of a data repository into a format that a person uses. This could be text/numeric or graphical outputs sent to paper (or PDF) or often put into a spreadsheet like Microsoft Excel.

From there, a person will work with the information—either using it to directly influence their business activities and decisions (good job!) or doing additional manual data manipulation and analysis to reach the point where they can put the report to use (a possible opportunity for improvement).

....

What separates reporting from other information-sharing mechanisms is that once the report is created, information does not flow directly back into the data repository.

....

Being a one-way communication mechanism, reports have their limitations, but this is not necessarily a bad thing. Compared to other options, it is a lot easier and faster to write a query to pull information from a database and export it into a PDF or Excel file. We can always establish information feedback loops further downstream that will recapture the data created from actions taken based on the reports.

Where things get dangerous is when we provide a report that is then manually integrated with a system outside our knowledge. It is perfectly reasonable to do this for exploratory and prototyping purposes, but many organizations fail to thoughtfully operationalize these early efforts. When that begins to happen frequently, do you know what that is called?

A big mess.

We apparently don't have an obtuse term for everything in data management! Having too many manual processes, Excel sprawl, or no clear knowledge of which reports are useful and which are worthless—these are real challenges faced by countless organizations. Many data analysts and data scientists spend considerably more time manipulating data than performing the analysis they were hired to do.

Reporting remains a fundamentally important capability today, and it will continue to have a role in organizations far into the future. Just like we must deliberately measure and improve balance across all DLF disciplines, reporting is part of keeping this balance. When considering how reporting should play a role, the first steps include quantifying the level of effort to produce the reports themselves, assessing the reports' usefulness, and determining their contribution to actual data value through business impacts.

Some organizations do not bother with this kind of meta-analysis of reporting because "There's no time!" This is the kind of misguided prioritization that causes things like Excel sprawl and the proliferation of useless reports in the first place.

....

We must break the cycle of simultaneously trying to run in every direction to address the many demands for our attention and energy!

....

Anyone who claims they do not have time to compile and measure performance data inevitably wastes a lot of time. How could they not? Do they have a magical sense of intuition that allows them to know all the relative value of their own behaviors? Can they even articulate what their value proposition, let alone value creation, really is? How do they ever improve without evidence of areas in which to improve? Are they claiming to be perfect? Are they the first perfect person? Are we that lucky to work alongside the world's first perfect person? Holy cow, should we order a cake or something? Does anybody know the number to the cake place?

Just seeing if you were paying attention amid all those questions, but the point is still valid. Once again, we can recall the simple virtuous cycle: measure, hypothesize, implement.

Reporting can be drastically improved if we simply hold ourselves accountable for understanding how people really use the reports we create.

Even with relatively simple reporting, optimization will likely pay huge dividends. Granted, turning off a report does not typically save a ton of money straightaway, but reducing the operational load, not to mention the support costs, adds up over time. Think of this basic reporting as low-hanging fruit. So how about we move up the tree a little?

Reporting is to graphical interfaces as photographs are to video games. Though a photograph tells a thousand words, a video game lets you battle Bowser. Which is more valuable? As any kid will tell us, video games are, no doubt, the way to go. It's not even close. Similarly, wouldn't everybody rather have a report they can do stuff with rather than just a sad, static page to look at? You betcha!

Data dashboards were amazing developments in the 1990s and early 2000s. They were graphical and easy-to-consume depictions of useful information. Some fancy ones even let us do a bit of filtering. This was groundbreaking at the time, because we hadn't had much exposure to this kind of information delivery mechanism—at least not without significant manual effort or large technology investment. Plus, being a stockbroker seemed supercool, and they were always shown looking at a bunch of screens with charts all over them.

Now we can do most of this stuff on a watch, let alone a phone.

Today's graphical interfaces are next level: drag-and-drop fields, report chart type selection on the fly, joining data sets at the application level, not to mention advanced aggregation and custom-function creation. All of it in real time! And all those, we can now do on a phone.

If we want to be bold and use a computer, this is where we can simply load files into memory and do all the analysis that used to require data warehouses and sophisticated in-memory aggregation accelerators cleverly called "cubes." That said, lots of times, it's still much simpler to use a data warehouse rather than files, driving more from the ease of administration versus a processing power constraint.

....

Our laptops today are plenty capable of storing and processing more data than many companies have.

....

Across many use cases, we live in a post-computing-horsepower-constrained world. If we are no longer constrained by our technical limitations, where does the bottleneck shift? Look in the mirror! We, the people, are now the weakest link! We are fundamentally limited by our abilities to consume and react to the data served to us at a pace that far exceeds our input capacities. Don't be too sad about it, though, because there is a silver lining to this cloud of disappointment.

Now that computing capacity universally exceeds our own, we get to compete on process design! Sure, that may not seem all that exciting, especially since so many of our organizations are so dreadfully bad at creating efficient processes. But it must be better now that we do not need to wait six months for that new server rack to arrive. We can design, implement, redesign, and reimplement many times over! There's that simple virtuous cycle sneaking in yet again.

As reporting has evolved alongside technology advances, it is becoming more visually oriented. Visualization tools enable analysts and other information workers to curate stories that can be presented to the end data consumers. These are like slideshows of interactive charts that help highlight the most interesting findings but also allow the end user to interact with them just as if they started with a blank screen in the interface. I've been involved with many presentations that use these tools, and very few other data delivery mechanisms can reach the top of the org chart with comparable pop.

Because of their grass-roots-through-executive-level reach, reporting and graphical interfaces should be among the top priorities for nearly all organizations. They are quite simply too powerful to be left on the bench. Even SQL-fluent individuals like myself will accomplish more by leveraging the incredible power of reporting and visualizations.

Before moving on, it's worth noting that there is a newer breed of ad hoc data wrangling and visualization tools that bypass the bigger ETL and data warehouse dynamics, often temporarily or as a proof of concept. Using these tools, single individuals without programming backgrounds can execute an entire data value chain without additional help! In some organizations, this is considered bad, with "shadow IT" a common term to describe perceived nonapproved technology use.

Shadow IT happens when some part of the business decides it has had enough of IT not giving them what they need, so they take matters into their own hands and just do it themselves! This can be things like unauthorized reporting and dashboard tools (like Tableau), using unsecured personal devices for business purposes, or even setting up stand-alone Amazon Web Services accounts.

....

Data leaders love to find shadow IT, as it is evidence of folks who are willing to break the rules to create data value. Their tactics may need some adjusting, but their hearts are in the right place!

....

Based on our understanding of data value, to some extent, we should embrace the people willing to push past the policies holding them back. If the net outcome is positive, what do we have to fear? Or is this a setup? Perhaps it is a valid perspective of one side of the story, whereas in the next section, we will balance it with an equally compelling perspective from the other side.

INTEGRATION

This is another of a few DLF disciplines that at first blush may seem to be in the wrong category. Shouldn't integration be in the access category? Well, no, because we would have put it there if that was where it should go. Sorry, that's not a helpful explanation. Let's try again.

The reason integration is in the use DLF category is that it is an automated data consumption mechanism. Consider this: a person reads a reporting output, analyzes it, and then performs some sort of action driven by the new knowledge. The most efficient improvement would be to eliminate the manual efforts entirely. If we can string together the data sources, analysis, and resulting actions, then people can spend their time on more valuable pursuits. Or maybe just go get a coffee; we won't judge.

Determining the algorithms and specific business process automation falls into the impact category, but systems integration represents the early stages where we need various independent systems to share basic information to ease data consumption and use. Thinking back to the previous section's unidirectional reporting discipline, doesn't integration, with its bidirectional data flows, seem like a more complete approach?

Here is a real-world example: There is a city undertaking a multimillion-dollar effort to replace its old-school streetlights in the city with more energy-efficient, smart LED lights. In addition to the energy savings, smart lights can be centrally controlled and actively monitored, so the system is aware of light outages before a citizen needs to call it in.

When city workers use the centralized smart lighting interface, they can obviously see information that pertains to the lights, since this information was generated by the lighting system itself. The folks building this system also thought it would be useful to have some information about electrical circuits, which are tracked separately in the transportation department's graphical information system (GIS) database. The GIS data was sent to the smart lighting application via a system integration.

Though it didn't directly automate a business outcome, this integration certainly saves time by allowing city personnel to access all the pertinent information through one user interface. Now if a citizen calls about a streetlight being out, city personnel can immediately check to see if its entire circuit is down and scheduled for repair or if this light has not been previously reported by the system and may be malfunctioning.

Systems integration is an important consideration for us because the best way to create actionable information may not be through a separate tool but to integrate data into something people are already using.

When our example GIS database was first created, nobody was thinking about the impact it might one day have in serving information to a futuristic smart lighting platform. The people building it only knew for sure that it might be called on to serve needs they couldn't currently predict. Good thing for our example city that they built it that way!

One of the most important concepts in the world of integration is that of creating highly aligned, loosely coupled system designs. The idea here is that when we have data, even with supercool data models and reporting capabilities, we don't know exactly what people are going to try to solve for or what specifically they are going to want to know in that process. Fortunately for us, this was figured out a long time ago.

Core to this kind of highly aligned, loosely coupled designs are APIs (application programming interfaces). These allow independent applications (installed, web, mobile, etc.) to interact with each other as needed without a specific process prescribing every step in a workflow. They lead to much greater flexibility, as data can be shared due to events like a user click, and new nodes and functionality can be added without disrupting the rest of the environment.

What gets fun with APIs is when we start building people process models using similar constructs. When people effectively serve as highly dynamic functions in a variable workflow but with standardized mechanisms for sharing information among one another, it just doesn't get better than that!*

Systems integration is typically not the highest priority consideration for us, but when it becomes important, it tends to become very important. It is also a function of seizing opportunities: rolling out new systems or making major changes can present us with avenues to work with information in innovative ways. We like that.

---

* To be fair, retirement is probably better than that. We'll let you know when we find out.

The best approach is to keep systems integration on the radar and find those unique opportunities to plug into other initiatives to add a lot of value for minimal additional cost or effort.

As data leaders, we achieve our greatest impacts when people do not even think about the tools. We want them thinking about the insights they can draw from data. Everything else is a distraction. The funny thing is that people really love distractions.

OPERATIONS

Operations is a simple word that quickly gets complex in its application. To start, it is everything an organization does to execute on its mission. If the organization is a charity, its mission is likely to help some group of people. If it is a bank, it is to help customers with some money to have more money or at least hold on to the money they had at the start. A sports franchise wants to entertain people enough to sell seats at a ballpark, branded merchandise, TV advertising, etc.

These examples of *business* operations can break down into the specific missions of different groups within the organizations: Sales gets the deals done, finance makes sure to get the money, manufacturing builds the product, and the technology group says no. Haha, just seeing if you are paying attention. The technology group buys and builds a bunch of tools and infrastructure to support all these other operations functions.

So where does *data* fit into all this? Quickly reread the last two paragraphs and think about where data plays a role in those. You'll discern that data is *everywhere* in various business operations, but the operations of data are even bigger than that!

In our data leadership world, operations will stretch over a variety of areas including data movements to connect technology systems, business processes that deliver on department-level missions like noted above, technology development, governance of data and processes, and even the core business operations of our organizations!

While there are nuanced differences in the various forms of operations, the functionality of all the operational areas are similar enough that this DLF operations lens will help us evaluate any or all of them that apply. The best data leadership efforts of any kind will become useless if we fail to establish appropriate standard processes around them. The goal here is developing productive, data-focused, operational structures to support data-related services *within* the data-related endeavors themselves.

....

We need to think about how data contributes to each of the operational functions of our organizations, and we also need to manage data operations like it is a core function of our organizations.

....

We must get our internal teams functioning well before we can reasonably hope to evolve the rest of our companies. While data people need to be given ongoing attention and new challenges to be fulfilled and satisfied in their career, data itself works similarly, but instead of career satisfaction, data must be nurtured to drive meaningful business outcomes.

Think of data having a career ambition of creating as much data value as it can. It goes to work, sitting in its database table, hoping one day to serve in the SQL query of its dreams. Occasionally it is called on, and the data performs its duties with vigor and aplomb. But what if the data is treated poorly, stored in underpowered databases with poorly defined data models and lacking indexes and simple metadata management? In this case, data responds slowly, with time-outs and data quality issues much more likely to occur.

People and data: we're not so different after all.

The idea of being "done" with data is like being "done" with human resources. It is never going to happen.

This is what this whole operations discipline is about: giving data the ongoing nurturing it needs to perform once the initial project is over. We can't assume that data will be fine if left alone. It will decay and subsequently perform poorly when we need it.

Let's break it down a bit.

- *Support* is how we respond to others who need us to help them. Calls for help often come in the form of emails or phone requests to fix something that is broken or build some capability that doesn't already exist. We probably need to track these requests and their resolutions and provide a mechanism to convert the bigger requests into projects. In smaller shops, the formality is probably going to be lesser, since we would often find ourselves spending time just recategorizing things that we will ultimately have to fix ourselves anyway. In larger environments, we may have access to a support team to manage basic requests, and our higher-level folks can focus a greater percentage of their time on solving more challenging problems.

- *Operations* is how our teams function in going about our business. Data teams can be a bit funky, since we will have highly technical (sometimes highly specialized) people who will need to play nicely with far-less-technical business subject matter experts. Throw in project managers, business analysts, and data scientists and analysts, and we have quite the motley crew. Especially when we think about how many data-centric folks have chosen this career due to their preference for talking with machines rather than people (no judgment here—I'm with you!). But add to all this that many folks will have "day jobs" above and beyond their participation in our data endeavors, and we have a big challenge in front of us.

- *DevOps* is a scary term that we threw in so that you knew we were serious about this stuff! Actually, DevOps is part development and part operations (another great term!), with the intent to maintain a better chain of custody for data responsibilities. This is why I started with a joke, as this topic gets a bit heavy. In short, if we must support and operate what we build, we will be motivated to build things better. This can be particularly true in the data space because the interdependencies are abundant.

- *DataOps* is like DevOps but for the data. Yes, I realize that sounds patronizing, and I do apologize for that. But if we consider it more closely, it gets more interesting. DataOps helps us do data management activities, represented by several data leadership disciplines, in ways more like we manage code for applications that are developed by teams of people. It needs to be iterative, meaning we improve things the more we do it. But if the organization hasn't developed a comfort with the fact that data is imperfect and can be used now but still improved later, then DataOps is going to meet an extra level of resistance compared with DevOps.

People are more comfortable with applications having bugs than they are with data being imperfect. Though this is directly addressed later in the context of data quality, our data operations lens should recognize that we can't always adopt for data what is accepted with other technology items. For example, if a web page won't load quickly or an application has downtime, people will accept those more easily than if a data update is half complete, resulting in reports showing unexpected results.

The challenge has historically been that to develop data outputs like reports, we needed information from our actual business systems (called "production systems and data"), but we also needed a safe place in which to work. This often resulted in duplicating data into a separate development environment, increasing complexity and potential errors along with significant costs. Now, since data can often be staggeringly large, doing all this back-and-forth is no longer reasonable. DataOps gives us a way to keep the data in production systems but with a safe place to develop data capabilities and then test and release features back into production systems in a safe and consistent way.

Hopefully the above descriptions help make sense of our catchall operations bucket and begin to make the case that these should be considered carefully and given an appropriate amount of attention if we want our data efforts to be sustainable in the long term.

....

Operations is an area, like data governance, where we should expect each hypothetical dollar of investment to be returned to the organization at least three times over in productivity enhancements.

....

A minimum threefold ROI is a rule of thumb that executives often use to quickly sort projects possibly worth attention versus those that are not. The thinking is that people are generally too optimistic, so when they claim threefold, a twofold return is a more probable outcome in the real world. Resources are scarce, and the disruptive nature of any significant change should at least double the amount of investment in return, whereas anything lower than a twofold return can be accomplished by less risky investments. It's this kind of thinking we need to be ready to overcome if we want our productivity improvement efforts to be seen as good investments.

A good rule of thumb is to try to find opportunities to hit a minimum of a fivefold return. It's not that hard to find when your organization has fundamental challenges with data-driven operations. The amount of your opportunity will determine how much you push into operations capabilities, but it should not be overlooked. Doing data in an ad hoc way has natural limitations, and as we transition to the impact DLF category, our focus shifts more and more toward repeatable, scalable, data-driven outcomes of real value. Data value, if it were a metal, would be gold.*

---

* If it were a medal, also gold. Convenient!

10

IMPACT: MAXIMIZE DATA VALUE

IT'S ALL ABOUT THE BUSINESS, BABY

It seems that many data-related initiatives are rooted in the belief that if we create something that people use, data value will be the inevitable outcome. This is wrong! Gaining *adoption*, getting people to use what you are delivering for valuable business actions, is a necessary step in creating data value, but it is not sufficient on its own. People can use data all day long but accomplish nothing meaningful in the end.

....

If we want to truly maximize data value, we must create a strong and deliberate connection between all DLF categories and the business outcomes we hope to affect.

....

Data leaders recognize that we can't leave value creation to chance, and that is what the entire DLF impact category is about. This category will not only help us fine-tune our data value–generating efforts, but it will help us build credibility within our organizations by quantifying the amount of value we create. This then feeds the business engagement activities that will amplify people's participation and the corresponding data value they create.

QUANTIFICATION

We cannot overstate the importance of measuring. Sustaining data value creation relies on taking measurements and responding to those measurements. When we talk about quantification, we are looking to use measurements, metrics, and key performance indicators to understand our business performance.

The most useful understanding may be aligned to real value by tracking revenues, costs, or risk management, but more often it will be looking at the performance of data value's building blocks as a proxy for the ideal quantification of real business value. While we might like to know *exactly* how much we improved sales through more detailed customer prospecting metrics, the fact that it led to a 20 percent increase in meeting acceptance rate is a positive sign along with an overall sales increase of 10 percent. We don't know exactly how meeting acceptance turns into real sales, but we know it must be a good thing, right?

While we prefer to tie our efforts directly to data value, sometimes measuring this is so difficult that we are better off using easily measured but imperfectly correlated metrics to evaluate our success.

Before moving forward, let's clarify some terminology. Do note that these definitions may vary somewhat across organizations but should at least loosely align:

- *Measurements*: Data, in the form of a number or state description, reflecting a truth about an object or process observation. Measurements can change over time and can have correlations to business outcomes. They may or may not have relationships to anything that can be controlled and may be internally or externally created. Simple examples include temperature, quantity, length, weight, brightness, and cost.

- *Metrics*: Measurements that are compiled with a comparative purpose in mind. If we see that last month, our car dealership sold 50 percent of the monthly total cars in the last three days, whereas typically it is only 20 percent, we may find it reasonable to investigate whether this was due to behaviors of our sales staff, availability of cars, holidays or other customer activity factors, or a new advertising campaign. Metrics help drive questions but typically don't deliver a direct opinion.

- *Key Performance Indicators (KPIs)*: KPIs are a special kind of metrics that we exert influence over. Response rates, sales goals, customer satisfaction—these are high-powered artifacts that can show us whether we are doing well or badly relative to an established target in metrics that we have some measure of control over. To create target values and ranges, we may employ scientific benchmarking against industry norms or use the less scientific approach of a manager's experience-driven whimsy.

Quantification is the foundation of data value. We can build some fantastic capabilities on these concepts, but if we find ourselves in an organization getting serious about data but lacking these fundamentals, we know we have some serious work to do. The ability to build on these basic quantification techniques is why we advocate for everyone to first start measuring and understanding today's truths before trying to change everything.

All the technology in the world can't solve a paradoxical equation, which is exactly what we create when we want to measure progress with an undefined starting point.

We will never be successful if we cannot measure the impact we have made. These concepts should seem straightforward by now, though in practice, quantification can get out of hand quickly. We do not have to be rock-star data scientist unicorns to do this stuff. We just need to measure, hypothesize, implement, and *repeat*. We can pepper in the complexity over time, which will make things easier for people learning along with us too.

It is not hard to find things to measure, especially if our business processes are creating data that is (or can be) stored in databases. The measurements in those cases are already there, but we will want to push them further. We should identify which business activities are not currently throwing off or capturing data effectively and how we might change that. It may require new sensors and IoT technologies or tweaks to business processes, but there is always a way.

Any half-decent manager should support better visibility into these things, but if we must play some politics, it is usually worth it. We should never forget that measuring processes, outputs, and efficiencies often sounds like oversight to folks and can be interpreted as a threat. These fears are often overblown but sometimes are perfectly justified. Especially in industries with longer histories and less culture of data-driven evaluations, we should tread carefully when advocating for rapid change.

It is preferable to have underutilized data rather than lose data that we may need someday, so we should at least make sure we're measuring and capturing data whenever we can. Once we establish measurements, building toward metrics and KPIs is more evolutionary. These will be pulled into existence by efforts in the other DLF disciplines, and we can be a little more patient on those.

The worst mistake is to miss out on worthwhile quantification by failing to capture and save data that will otherwise disappear forever.

We better prioritize this discipline accordingly, especially since we will not get very far in the rest of our DLF impact efforts without a core competency in this area. For any imaginable data program, this DLF discipline is likely a top five consideration. Once the triage stage is passed and we have baseline quantification, we can lower it on the list in favor of other value-building efforts, but this is one discipline that should always remain in our field of vision.

DATA SCIENCE

This discipline could have just as easily been labeled *statistics*, but then nobody would read it. Isn't it hilarious that data science was coined as a sexy rebranding of statistics, not unlike how people started eating Chilean sea bass only after they changed the name from Patagonian toothfish? Maybe *hilarious* is overstating it, but as we've learned throughout this book, data jokes only get so good.

Out of principle, we're also fighting the instinct to call this section data science, since that term overlaps several of our DLF disciplines. This whole branding of data science is fascinating.

A layperson's definition of data science seems to be "fancy stuff with numbers *and* programming that probably only people smarter than me can do." The rational explanation of this is people are irrationally afraid of both numbers *and* programming. In other words, data science can be *everything* we individually don't understand about data! This enigmatic aura leads data scientists to command high salaries, because they know important things that the rest of us don't. What are they? We could tell you, but then you'd be a data scientist too, and they can't afford to pay us both this much.

Data science gains its superpowers from the vaguely intimidating but tough to qualify responsibilities that vary considerably among different companies and teams.

After dozens of moments of contemplation, we have reached an important decision: employment economics be darned! We're going to throw back the curtain and teach you the secrets of data science anyway!

Starting with basics, once we have measurements and perhaps even metrics and KPIs, we will quickly move beyond the line chart ("Look! It goes up!") and into more sophisticated analyses.

For those of us who once took a Statistics 101 course, this is a refresher of what we learned and immediately forgot about after the final. For those who haven't had the opportunity to forget a basic statistics curriculum, this is a very simple introduction that we'll move on from quickly.

Statistics relies on things called r values and p values, and the resulting correlation leads to an estimate and a plus or minus percentage level of confidence that our results are not mere coincidence. These are the humble beginnings of all the fancy data science that comes later.

Predictive modeling takes regressions and flips the direction so that we can try to, ahem, predict the future through what happened in the past. Have we seen those disclaimers from financial companies? "The contents herein should be used for information purposes. Past performance does not guarantee future results." But isn't that *exactly* what they are trying to do? Who are they kidding?

This is spinning a bit now, so we need to keep moving forward. Like all the topics here, we are just scratching the surface, and statistics as a discipline is as old and deep as they come.

....

A good strategy in the early days of a data program is to hitch our wagons to one or more numbers people who can dive into the details but may struggle connecting their research to actions that improve business outcomes.

....

Since connecting data efforts to business outcomes is what data leaders do best, this is exactly the kind of partnering that data leaders should be looking to forge. We do not all need to be experts at doing the analysis, but if we can take the outputs and effect meaningful change, then everybody wins!

The priority we assign to this DLF discipline will depend on a couple of factors. First, can we do some of this analysis ourselves, or is there somebody in the organization with this skill set? It is a lot easier to source this internally than to hire from the outside or pay a high-priced consultant who does not know your business. Second, how ready is our data for this kind of analysis? If we have material data quality challenges or our measurements are inconsistently captured, then the more complicated regression analysis will not be as fruitful.

Data science in any context brings together programming and statistics functions to drive analytical insights. As data science has matured, the complexity and power of these foundations have increased exponentially. This is where machine learning enters the picture. Along with its closely related counterpart artificial intelligence (AI), these are two of today's hottest data terms, and for good reason. These are how we can take enormous data sets and some generic notion of a pattern we'd like to investigate and utilize the effectively unlimited computing power now available to us, whittling it all down to actionable insights.

These two subjects are closely related but not quite the same:

- *Artificial Intelligence:* a branch of computer science attempting to build machines capable of intelligent behavior.
- *Machine Learning:* the science of getting computers to act without being explicitly programmed.[1]

Machine learning sounds a little more approachable, right? This should be our mentality—let's use the machines to help us solve data challenges to improve our businesses without necessarily trying to create sentient computer beings.

Lest we think AI is about trying to create life, we should read the above definition a little closer. AI is about trying to make the machines behave intelligently. Many of us have the same challenge with our kids! We do not need computers to think like people; we just need them to clean up their rooms before bedtime without a big fight. That is, the benefit of AI systems is that they are generally rational, whereas children are highly irrational, especially when they are hungry or tired.

Based on our small but strongly correlated analogy, if we need something done without having to tell them a million times, give us less theoretically capable but way more rational AI robots any time!

What is the problem with emotional, irrational children? They grow up to become emotional, irrational adults. These are the people on our teams and even us! This presents challenges for data leadership, regardless of what we do. Even with the best outputs, the clearest conclusions, and highly predictable business benefits, we have to hope that people will do the right thing in the end. Sadly, we cannot even be sure that people will act in their own best interests, let alone the company's!

There has been a lot of chatter lately about AI taking over and destroying the world someday. That may or may not even be possible, but it is inherently frightening. Why is that? Wouldn't it be a better idea to entrust the future of the world to highly intelligent, rational machines? Of course not! That's crazy!

Though people are emotional and irrational and this will hurt our productivity from time to time, the complementary benefit is that we can have empathy.

People are unreliable, error prone, and flaky—especially when hungry. And even though we are supposed to be reliably selfish, we don't even do that consistently. Sometimes we care about things that have no direct correlation to our own well-being, acting in opposition to our own self-interests because of a story that tugs on our heartstrings or when giving our lunch to a homeless person will clearly help them more than us. Throughout history, people have willingly died for causes they believed in, and this phenomenon could only be driven by irrational, emotional, empathetic, flawed, beautiful human beings.

And yes, we also do irrational things that are intentionally harmful to ourselves or others. Sadly, we often do this without any rational reason at all. The pendulum is always swinging back and forth. And this kind of unpredictability is a tough thing to program.

Maybe none of this will impact our decisions to begin employing machine learning in our data programs, but with the pace of technology continuing to evolve ever more quickly, this may be a more valid concern than we think.

So where does this DLF discipline fit into our balanced approach to data leadership? Normally, we would probably advocate saving this one for a little bit further into our journey. It is usually better to get the basics right before doing the fancy stuff, but there is a caveat: if your executives read something and are now excited to pursue an advanced machine learning strategy, we have one word: yes!

....

Machine learning and related areas can drive excitement and impact but will be less effective without strong business-side interest and foundational data capabilities, like quantification.

....

When we have strong business-side interest, we must do whatever we can to nurture it. It's harder to build business interest in data than implement any specific data technology. When we are lucky enough to have people's attention, we had better take advantage of it.

One factor changing the feasibility of machine learning is that cloud platform providers like Amazon Web Services have rolled out services to make these tools more accessible than they previously were. Entry-level costs are now approachable for pretty much any company looking to start working with these capabilities. This is both awesome and terrifying when we consider the number of people who now have access to potentially create "evil" AI or at least the number of people with companies with the data analytics potential to kick our butts in the competitive marketplace.

The above technically connotes the literal meaning of *awesome*, which often has a component of fear. But most of the time, people think "awesome" is just another word for "great," so we felt clarification was needed. We also feel that sometimes these anecdotes are a way to avoid writing more substantive content. How is that procrastination helping us? It's not. And then this becomes yet another example of silly, irrational, human behavior. See what we did there?

If our folks are already well into data use and clamoring for more depth of data insights, now we're talking! Remember not to take an if-we-build-it-they-will-come mentality here, and when to invest significantly in this area will come into focus at the right time.

AUTOMATION

Automation is taking this rich tapestry of data capabilities we've covered throughout the DLF and applying them to directly drive business impacts! Remember all that stuff in the last section about irrational people not doing what the data tells them to do? That can all be history if we automate the processes entirely!

....

Automation can do awesome things when coupled to machine learning.

....

This is the dream: When we provide data capabilities to people, we help make their business decisions and activities ever more efficient. We measure, hypothesize, implement, and repeat until some of the decisions and activities can be automated entirely. That frees up personnel to take on new decisions and activities that are less predictable.

Many of these automation efforts are comparatively not that complicated, and the actual decision-making processes and resulting activities are often strikingly simple. Today, many information workers spend a startling amount of their time doing relatively low-value work that can be automated significantly, if not completely.

....

Look for automation opportunities where people have already built their own data solutions and automations, often haphazardly and with tools that are easy to use but difficult to scale or maintain.

....

For example, Microsoft Access is never the right answer for a long-term solution a business relies on. It can do a lot of things quickly, and the skill set necessary to use it is not as technical as comparable tools. It's a fantastic option for creating proofs of concept or a temporary database to organize a potluck. Unfortunately, what makes it so user friendly also makes it dangerous for many of the use cases where we see it incorrectly applied.

Without getting too technical, Microsoft Access combines too many aspects of a full-fledged database system. The data storage layer, computational engine, and user interface are all wrapped together and stored in the same files. This makes the output a security nightmare: so easy to share, but also easy to lose. Access database files are often unintentionally duplicated and result in people relying on versions that are no longer the same. The design decisions made in the software lead to an unwieldy, risk-laden tool with brittle artifacts prone to corruption and data loss.

A simple approach is to find anybody using Microsoft Access in an inappropriate context and then have them replace it with a proper enterprise-grade tool. Sounds a little harsh, right? Using Microsoft Access for a production workload is like a hospital replacing all its doctors with touch screens and a popular self-diagnosing website. Microsoft Access is not the right tool for the task at hand.

This is not to say that people using Microsoft Access have bad intentions; they are just unaware that the software fills no enterprise functionality purpose in an organization. It simply fills a gap in knowledge of the appropriate tools. With data professionals on the case, we can bring Microsoft Access artifacts into a true database environment, along with the governance and data protections that will inevitably be necessary for something people cared enough to go out and build on their own. We can use SQL Server if we like Microsoft or use something like PostgreSQL or MariaDB if we prefer something free.

Another fruit-on-the-ground example is Excel hell. People love to use Microsoft Excel for analysis because it is so flexible. It seems that Excel has a sizable lead as the most heavily used data analysis tool anywhere, probably by a factor of three. People love Excel, and rightfully so—it is an absolute gift to do basic iterative analysis and arrive at data-driven conclusions. The problem occurs when people start using it for repetitive tasks.

Once an Excel file is created, edited, and eventually shared, there should be a rule that the file is locked permanently and can never be edited again. If we want to make a new version, it must be created as a separate file. This would help keep us from losing data, which inevitably happens with Excel in the wild. It would not help us keep from making a huge mess, which also inevitably happens whenever Excel is freely used.

Once Excel is used to create something that will need to be

reproduced, it should be adapted into a more formal mechanism, driven by consistent data sources. Interactive dashboard tools are great at this. We should use them instead!

In case this section feels like Microsoft bashing, understand that the criticisms are not that Microsoft is making bad tools; it's quite the opposite! Microsoft's tools are so capable and accessible to folks that people can use them to accomplish a great deal. The downside is that people can build so much, so quickly, that their creations grow to a point where they become too difficult to maintain, and the resulting costs and/or risks degrade the investment returns of these efforts to the point where they consume more resources than they create benefits.

....

Data leaders must provide the right tools, but the goal is to automate business processes entirely when possible!

....

People want to use data to improve business decisions and activities, but they can't do it all themselves. Some business processes will never be fully automated. But we see so many business processes out there that are just people going through the motions because they don't know there is another way. This is a boring, sad existence for any person brilliant enough to work in our organizations. Let's help give them something more interesting to do, and then everybody wins!

MONETIZATION

We have already talked exhaustively about data value, and we have discussed so many disciplines that work together to create data value. We get that most of this is complicated stuff, both conceptually and in what it takes to realize value through the coordination of everything. Well, compared to most, this one is simple.

Monetization is about turning data into money by emphasizing the increasing revenue piece of the data value equation.

The most obvious way to achieve data monetization is to sell data to others who find it valuable. This could take the form of selling email addresses to other companies that want to market to our customers. Or it could be that upstream vendors want to better understand their market, so our data could inform them on how we ultimately serve the end consumers, and the vendor could respond by making more customized products.

People tend to not like being commoditized, so the example of selling raw data can particularly raise privacy concerns. When monetizing data, we must be careful not to do something that could anger our customer base. The financial impact from that will likely far outweigh anything we would make through monetization efforts.

Let us think about the second example for a moment—providing data to vendors for analysis. Assuming these insights are useful to the vendor, would it be valuable to them if we could save them the trouble of doing the analysis and deliver the insights to them directly? This would save them effort and get at what they care about most, all while protecting the details of our customers' information.

Not unlike data quality, monetization opportunities exist on a curve that shows the level of effort and resulting value alongside how removed we are from the atomic data. "Atomic data" is a common data warehousing term that means the data cannot be further reduced. For example, a product order is made up of one to many items and related quantities. An order is not typically an atomic data point, but the order line items are.

The power of monetization lies not purely in the data but in the analytics that drive business outcomes. It is one thing to have data—all organizations do. But how many are making the most of the data they already have? Is the hypothesis that more data will help them really the most reasonable conclusion? What everyone needs are answers, not just data. Any data monetization effort should be acutely aware of this.

....

No more pure measure exists for how much data value is created than dollars directly generated from the corresponding activities.

....

Monetization effectiveness can be a proxy for overall data value chain effectiveness. Dollars directly created from data efforts may tend to understate the truth, however, since efforts with direct effects also tend to residually impact other areas. This is even more true the more levels of abstraction we have. Advanced analysis is likely to have more wide-ranging implications than raw data alone.

The entire impact category represents the capstone of the data value chain, which we as data leaders are charged with maximizing. This is where we can review progress and identify improvements for the next iteration, completing the feedback loop and connecting us back to the beginning. In most of the areas we have covered so far, we will always welcome help; they largely orient to things we can accomplish more directly.

Once we get good things happening, though, we need to elevate beyond our direct impact and nurture behaviors which amplify data value. This is the purpose of the govern category, where we will look to build a culture that can grow data leadership to permeate every corner of our organizations—like how even a ridiculously small amount of glitter will expand into an infinite space which can never be fully cleaned up. Except in a good way.

CITATION

1 Lee Bell, "Machine Learning Versus AI: What's the Difference?," *Wired*, January 12, 2016, https://www.wired.co.uk/article/machine-learning-ai-explained.

11

GOVERN: SCALE RESULTS

BALANCED GROWTH WILL NOT HAPPEN BY ACCIDENT
The final DLF category is about governance, which is less concerned with the life cycle covered by the other four categories and more about aligning and accelerating how our organizations capitalize on the data capabilities we build.

The film *Field of Dreams* apparently continues to ruin the minds of data and technology professionals, decades after its release. In this classic '80s movie, a ghostly voice keeps saying, "If you build it, they will come," in reference to building a baseball field in the middle of an Iowa corn farm. And yes, the '80s were weird.

This concept, "If we build it, they will come," unequivocally does not apply to data and analytics.

There are countless reports, interactive dashboards, and even entire data warehouses that go completely unused or significantly underutilized in organizations across the world. Some of them may have flawed designs, while others were built exceedingly well.

Ignoring those that missed the mark completely, what went wrong? Why wouldn't people fully embrace the data and analytics capabilities given to them? Don't they realize the power at their fingertips?

Obviously, they don't realize the power at their fingertips! People are busy working! They are not sitting around waiting for us to save them with data. Simply building things and making them available is only part of the answer. We are going to need to explain, reach out, convince, teach, market, package, adjust, justify, prove, and ultimately sell our solutions to people to make the changes to achieve data value. Try saying that five times fast! Hard enough to say and even harder to make happen!

It's up to data leaders to introduce people to data-related capabilities and ensure they have all the tools they need to be successful. We must realize and accept that nobody owes us a sale.

Now that we're all worked up, let's get into the details of how to connect these amazing creations to the people who don't care (yet) that we built them!

Sometimes we must take our medicine. Data governance is the nasty green syrup that tastes bad but will help our organizations put data assets to use at scale. This is where we find compliance and regulatory mandates, standards and policies, privacy, acceptable use, and a host of other things that we *have* to do but we may or may not *want* to do.

These many things also happen to be covered in truly exhaustive and excruciating detail by countless other data governance–related books. Lucky for you, we will not go down that rabbit hole here, but rest assured that without reading at least a couple of these books, we will have a significant gap in this domain of knowledge. Rather than rehash what so many other resources cover at length, what we will spend a little more time on here is the strategic aspects of data governance.

STRATEGY

Governing data implies a perspective of how data assets and use should be coordinated to achieve the targets of a data strategy. But there is no such thing as a stand-alone data strategy. Data strategy is a highly aligned, tactical manifestation of business strategy and cannot be created nor exist independently.

If data value is the desired outcome (it is!), data strategy and data governance exist to interpret and coordinate actions driven by business strategy.

Recall that data value is created by impacting what a business does, and a business figures out what to do based on their business strategy. But what even is a business strategy?

Business strategy is what executives come up with during a special retreat, often at a place that sounds made up. Islands are popular, so we're told. One rarely hears of the transformative executive business strategy retreat that happened in Cleveland.

Let's break down the "strategies" without getting distracted by dissing Cleveland:

- *Business strategy* is what ostensibly guides the decisions, activities, and ultimately the performance of our organizations.
- *Data strategy* outlines how our data leadership efforts align with the business strategy. A data strategy will cover more specifics in the DLF disciplines that we intend to devote our energies toward and even outline a road map of projects and milestones that we intend to undertake and reach, respectively.
- *Data governance strategy* is the detailed prioritization and resource allocation of the governance DLF disciplines (strategy, change, adoption, and stewardship).

....

Governance is making the best activities happen, but *strategy* is figuring out which activities are most likely to have the biggest impact.

....

A data strategy that is not fundamentally driven by business strategy may undertake worthwhile pursuits, but their relevance to business outcomes will be relegated to chance. This is wasteful, no doubt. But what if our business does not have a formal business strategy?

Giving up is not an option! And frankly, this is the case more often than we would hope. That said, nothing changes, except now instead of coming up with a data strategy, we first need to come up with what we think the business strategy is, even if nobody has written it down yet. Perhaps our executives are more operationally focused and are not actively developing larger-scale change initiatives that data might drive. If they need some help defining what the strategy might be, then we will have to be the ones to do it.

As data leaders, we cannot let any barriers stand in our way, even if it means taking responsibility for articulating our companies' overall business goals. We will not decide the strategy for the executives, but we *will* document it. At minimum, we're going to have to interpret the details ourselves, since few business strategies clearly articulate whether "double EBITDA* in the next three quarters" means we focus on improving quality in our customer master data or on delivering more capable sales dashboards.

Business strategies can be difficult to articulate, since executives operate at such a high level they may no longer directly see (or appreciate) the complexities of doing frontline business processes. This means that a business strategy can feel disconnected from reality when driven purely from the top down.

Data leaders should be able to connect operational truths to the strategic vision at any level. In theory, this means we should

---

*EBITDA = earnings before interest, taxes, depreciation, and amortization. It is intended to better measure how well your business is doing at its core functions without all the funky stuff that throws off the numbers.

be able to document any missing levels of the business strategy, even when the business strategy itself is only implied and not explicitly defined.

> **If nonexecutive data leaders attempt to document business strategy and it turns out to be wildly incorrect, we can count on the executives letting us know.**

Hmm. This whole notion of documenting the truth around us and then soliciting feedback and validation sounds awfully familiar. What could that be?

Right! This is a metadata management effort in disguise! Capture what the business strategy *is*, and then we can have a meaningful conversation about what our data strategy *should be*.

To develop an excellent data strategy, we will also need to have a good grasp of our current capabilities from throughout the DLF. Once we have a baseline understanding of where we are, then we can begin to set a strategy to make changes. This is just like what we do in the refine category, but instead of operating at the data level, we are at the overall process level.

It isn't enough to simply execute the process and expect optimal outcomes. Putting effort into improving the process will lead to greater improvements every time. This hints at the philosophical core of the agile methodology and DevOps. Rather than attempt to paraphrase the lessons, I recommend *The Phoenix Project* as an excellent resource to understand how information process design plays a pivotal role in everything we do with data. The book is about software development, but it really applies to anyone trying to catalyze transformative changes in an organization.

Once we understand our business strategy and can anchor it to our current data capabilities, we are in good shape. We will be able to craft a data strategy that is achievable and has measurable outcomes that will deliver real business impact. This is powerful stuff!

A data strategy can be as simple as this: we're going to measure how long it takes from an external data source being updated until we have made the data available in our system, and our data ingestion team's success will be determined by improvements to that metric. Or it can be more complicated, like improving customer relationships through capturing and evaluating net promoter score, which is a metric designed to understand how likely a customer is to recommend your organization to someone else.

This is also why surveys often ask whether you are likely to recommend a business to someone else. They can be useful, but they are often misused. I laughed out loud when my garbage collecting service, for which I have no choice whatsoever, asked me if I would recommend them to my friends and family. Yes, absolutely, I am extremely satisfied with my garbage removal and looking forward to telling my friends and family to use a service they can't use even if they wanted to. C'mon, not everything needs to elicit passion.*

A well-designed data strategy accomplishes two things. First, it presents a clear vision of the future we're working toward;

---

*And yes, I understand the irony, as I get worked up about pretty much everything.

it answers *why* we are doing this. This is essential to helping motivate the folks whose efforts we will seek to make it happen. Second, our data strategy must answer *how* we will achieve this future state vision.

> **The reality is that data strategy is a bridge between business strategy and data value.**

Our data strategy must provide enough clarity into specific actions to give people hope that we will be able to transform strategic vision into real vision. And some pragmatic data governance doesn't hurt either.

Data strategy is the most common term, so we've used it throughout this section, but one could also think of this area as data leadership strategy. It is all about identifying opportunities for data to influence change to improve our business outcomes. Data strategy is more aligned with the impact of data insights directly, whereas a data leadership strategy takes a comprehensive approach to how we're structuring people, process, technology, and data to work in tandem to drive change. Change is the common denominator. Let's dive in.

CHANGE

On the heels of a rock-solid data strategy, our focus shifts to getting the real work moving. A data strategy by itself accomplishes nothing. We need a detailed coordination plan to help these five DLF categories and twenty DLF disciplines move forward in harmony.

A classical orchestra is an apt analogy here. The categories represent a class of instruments, like strings or percussion. The individual disciplines are a specific instrument type, like violins or xylophones. The overall amount of effort we put into specific disciplines are the number of players of that instrument. And change management is the sheet music coordinating everyone's playing.

And guess who the conductor is?

Data leaders do the work when nobody else will, and we take full responsibility for the success or failure of every data-related endeavor in our organizations, whether we have control of it or not.

Though there may be countless reasons why we do not achieve our data goals, we never have a valid excuse. Our role as data leaders is to make maximum data value happen. Full stop.

Many of us may find that we do not even have good access into the existing change management capabilities in our organizations. Project management offices (PMOs) are often their own domains, far removed from data concepts, and often held at arm's length from our IT friends. We may need to find a way into their club, or maybe in a worst-case scenario, we can operate independently as a data-focused "shadow PMO."

That is not really an actual thing, but we somehow need to coordinate the many activities involved with creating data value. Let us assume that we have an ability to engage with the PMO. The first job is to figure out where their acute data challenges are and find a way to help. Chances are there are ways in which our interests align with their needs, and we might be able to leverage their coordination mechanisms to facilitate our data activities.

The head of our organization's PMO is among the most important people a data leader can befriend. We need to get things done, and even super inefficient PMOs with terrible leadership are going to get us further than trying the "shadow PMO" idea we discussed briefly above.

....

While we must break down barriers to transform our organizations, we should do it within reasonable parameters. It can be difficult to remain effective if we become known as wild cards.

....

Managing organizational change is an entire career path by itself, and our PMO experts are usually better at it than we data leaders are. Our goal should be to influence their priorities so they are considering the power of data to help the organization. After all, the mission of change management resolves to the same thing as data value: influencing the revenues, costs, and risk management of an organization.

ADOPTION

People are not going to understand what data can do unless we show them and then teach them what they need to know to repeat it themselves. If we can give them the opportunity to work with data and have the experience be positive and productive, then they will become more motivated to build on their initial skills and produce even better results.

....

An important goal is to build self-reinforcing systems that create their own momentum over time.

....

The first step in this is to introduce capabilities to people, even before the capabilities themselves are fully built. Wouldn't it be nice to get some insight into what people like and where the opportunities for improvement are before some grand unveiling that may unexpectedly miss the mark?

People will resist at the beginning. This is going to be true in any circumstance where the dreaded term "change" enters the picture. If we are going to push for people to change, we need to make it worth the hassle for them and for us. It is rarely worth crafting an extensive change initiative for minor benefits, but if we can pull together a bunch of benefits to justify a need for change, then it makes changing more reasonable to people.

Changing technology systems is easy: we just code some new stuff, hit a button, and like magic—changes complete! With adoption, though, we are asking people to change. We can't just wait for the spinning hourglass to stop. We need to give people reasons to do something different and an understanding of why it will be helpful to the organization and to them as individuals! Thus, within adoption, training and culture are central concepts to understand.

- *Training:* giving people instructions on how to perform specific activities or processes in the pursuit of creating data value.
- *Culture:* helping people infer general behavior patterns that create data value in appropriate ways for their roles.

One organization I worked with that did a good job with training and culture is a large school district that employs about forty-five thousand people. They had an IT organization a fraction of the size they reasonably should have had, but the leadership team were strong advocates for data analytics. They created a data working group that spanned across the entire organization and attracted over forty self-selecting participants to regular workshops. The working group leaders created training materials and online walkthroughs, and the results were impressive. Teachers were able to better understand grade distribution patterns in their classes compared to norms, and social workers could identify troubling absence patterns earlier, leading to earlier and more successful interventions. The data working group participants quickly made inroads using data analytics in their everyday work, and then they were able to spread the skills to others who were not formal data working group members.

This kind of train-the-trainer approach is essential to get widespread adoption. The organization in the above example had plenty of issues getting data consistency *across* all their schools, but they uniquely excelled at building data culture *within* individual schools. The folks in the workshops were excited to be learning SQL (SQL!) and were regularly taking what they were learning in the morning and applying it in their daily work by the afternoon. It was beautiful.

Now, we should all aspire to have that kind of training success, but it probably won't come easily. In fact, that same client had struggled for nearly a year to drive attendance and get the right format and participants, but they stuck with it. Something to be said for perseverance, certainly.

....

In our pursuit of creating data value, acting is more important than anything else.

....

Get out of the meeting room, find an opportunity to change things for the better, get the data dancing, and go make an impact! Let's find a way to get away from talking about working and start working! Meetings alone will never change how we work, and if we don't change how we work, we will create no data value. If we lead by example and create momentum through our actions, we can create a more quantitative culture inside our businesses.

The process of building adoption can take many forms, and the ones your organization needs most may not be immediately evident. There are also macro and microitems to consider. Individual departments or business units may need a very specific and deep data literacy for their folks, while other areas may need broad-based knowledge across a variety of data domains. But understanding what is going on within our organizations, just like our earlier discipline around context, is just the beginning. Inevitably, as we gain more knowledge, we will find some aspects of our data that we have opinions on and want those opinions to be consistently adopted throughout our businesses. This is what we data folks call "the big G": data governance.

Just kidding, nobody calls data governance "the big G." But they should. I will if you will.

We have touched on this in other sections, but just because we do something theoretically productive does not guarantee its actual positive impact on our organization. We must sell it—help people understand why their lives will be better off if they use what we've built.

IT organizations have typically done this poorly. They build *whatever* at the direction of *whomever*, and then once it is delivered, they generally leave it up to the business to make the most of it. The IT folks figure they will learn the rest of what they need to do via feature requests or bug reports. This is predicated on the flawed assumption that the business will communicate those needs back to them instead of complaining to each other that IT gave them another garbage solution.

Establishing real partnerships while still embracing a level of personal responsibility ultimately leads to the data value that we are looking to create. We also often find we do not have as much organizational control as we would like, so we resort to catching flies with honey! This means we use the powers of gentle persuasion to convince folks to help, use what we've built, buy some new tech, or pay our salaries.

....

Data leaders cannot possibly succeed by chucking responsibility over the fence to the business. We *are* the business!

....

When we encounter frustration in our businesses, it is not a wholly bad sign. Angry people are ready for change. They are in the fight, and they have not given up. If we can turn their anger and frustration toward hope and action, we can do anything!

Indifference, on the other hand, is a much tougher problem. Disengaged people simply do not care, so it becomes much more difficult to get them to act. We must somehow incentivize them to do more with data, but when they do not care about the shared benefits to the company, all we have is every individual's self-interest. Leveraging that can get expensive.

It's arguably wise to align our marketing and communications efforts to feed the self-interests of people who will do things to further our data goals. I've long said *The Little Red Hen* is one of the best business books around. It recounts the fable of a mother hen beginning to bake bread, asking for help from various characters from the stages of cultivating wheat through ultimately eating the bread. Nobody would help until it came time to eat, and then the hen tells everybody (except her adorable children) that they shall get none. The business lesson here is that if she led with "if you are going to want some bread, pick up the dang shovel," she probably would have gotten more help. Or perhaps the lesson is this: if you help, then maybe you'll get some bread. Or maybe you can probably steal the bread if she turns her back. Like I said, great book.

Despite the unclear lessons from the literary journey above, the problem is that people aren't all that great at doing things that optimize their overall self-interest. Motivating people, as we discussed early on, is not a simple endeavor. If we do not know what the optimal strategy to engage people is, we should focus on being the more appealing option compared to their next best alternatives. It helps if we are doing good things for them too, but we know this alone isn't the best motivator.

The activities that comprise the DLF should never be misrepresented as benefiting certain individuals if they won't. But some doughnuts and coffee at the meetings sure wouldn't hurt!

Incentives are the magic ingredients. A contest to see which department can drive the most revenue growth from data analytics may be a viable idea. Sharing cost reductions with employees is another common one. Even something as simple as public recognition or a bottle of wine can work wonders with things like metadata business glossary definition gathering.

The key is to give people something above and beyond when we ask them to go above and beyond.

How incentives should manifest in any organization is a nontrivial exercise, and the answers will vary. Most failed data programs did not deliberately design and coordinate their communications efforts. We cannot suffer that fate. Losing sight of this discipline risks *everything* else.

STEWARDSHIP

This is fittingly the last discipline we cover in the DLF, because for so many organizations, it is the triggering event behind doing data governance and other data management activities. Though we generally advocate an innovation-centric approach to data-driven change, being told by an auditor, a regulator, or any external entity that we must comply with something is often the main initial motivator for organizations. We can loosely group audit findings, certifications, and any other arbitrary rules we decide to follow in this compliance area.

....

Focusing on policy alone rarely leads to lasting data leadership.

....

An overemphasis on compliance is like when people memorize the answers for a certification test, pass it, and then subsequently fail because they aren't any good at what the certification said they could do. When we use this kind of thinking to spearhead data leadership, we will fall into the same trap but at an organization level. We may succeed in checking the auditor's box, but we will miss out on creating data value.

Remember how we've often said that data value is the only thing that matters? Compliance is a way to *potentially* create data value, but it is not the same thing as creating real data value. Complying with regulations allows us to mitigate risk and potentially increase revenues or decrease costs. Those are good things, and we should add them to the list of ways we create data value. But there is so much more potential here than simply passing a test!

....

If our organizations are asking for it, we should devote some energies to policy, because as much as we wish it weren't the triggering factor, it is where organizations often start their data leadership journeys.

....

We're going to try to expand everyone's horizons to see the true potential of data-driven change, but we also need to work with what we've got. And this is certainly better than starting with no support.

Well then, Mr. Policy-Pants, what do we do?

First, we need to know the specific sets of rules with which we must comply. Determining this may be a function of our compliance department, or it could fall to lawyers, risk management, or our finance and accounting folks. It will vary from organization to organization. Once we start digging into all this, it is certain to unveil a whole universe of headaches that we may, quite frankly, wish we never had to worry about.

A common example is the European Union's GDPR, which provides strict rules on how organizations can use and must protect information for any EU-covered person. While many Americans may think, "Who cares? That's not our problem," the fact is that any company that does business with an EU person must comply, even if it is on U.S. soil. In other words, if a person from the EU comes to visit our hotel, rents equipment from us, or hires us to paint their house, we may need to worry about GDPR.

Sure, we might question how the EU would be able to enforce these restrictions on a local company. They probably can't. But if we represent a larger business with global operations and deeper pockets, the EU may be much more likely to track us down.

When to fully comply with regulations and when to take our chances is more aligned to the security discipline in the access category, but from a governance point of view, we must find a way to align our organization's data efforts with the strategic decisions made as a business.

The GDPR is one example of a regulation that we could easily miss but may find that we unwittingly violated. If we have an unexpected and unintended data breach (aren't they all?), we may find that we are in violation of many regulatory constraints that we didn't even know about. Herein lies the fallacy that a check-the-box approach will ever be sufficient— they will always be adding boxes for us to check.

> **With true data leadership, we will be building the right organizational competencies to address the ever-increasing volume and variety of compliance mandates, often satisfying them prior to their existence.**

Data is becoming recognized as one of the most important assets an organization has, and our responsibilities as custodians of that data are increasing in kind. We must help our organizations manage the power and the risks of data due to market forces and the rules that we are required to follow. Data leaders should evolve beyond reacting to requests to taking a more proactive role in how our organizations address policy.

PART 3

DATA LEADERSHIP IN ACTION

12

THE DATA LEADERSHIP
FRAMEWORK IN ACTION

THE DLF IS A COMPASS MORE THAN A MAP

We have gone through the *why* and *what* questions of data leadership and the DLF, respectively. Now, we cover the *how*. And if you are thinking about the *who* and *when* questions, I will cover those two in this single sentence: *who* is "all of us," and *when* is "now and forever." See? Not everything with data is hard to understand.

Back to the *how*. The secret is we've already mostly covered it! It tracks back to the simple virtuous cycle: measure, hypothesize, implement, and repeat! This is the foundation of data value and thus the core of applying the DLF. Though I won't end this chapter after two relatively short paragraphs, I reasonably could. Since verbosity is next to godliness (I think the saying goes), let's illuminate this topic with a bunch more words.

We have now covered the DLF at its highest level, and it feels like we are barely getting started. The depth of each of the twenty DLF disciplines cannot be understated. Most could (and do!) have their own dedicated books focused on the specific subjects. In the context of data leadership, we have established a rudimentary understanding of what each of these is, but mastering them will take a lifetime.

Even career data management folks are not experts in everything. The strongest data professionals will typically have deep backgrounds in one to three of the DLF disciplines, meaningful experience in a dozen, and hopefully a hearty appreciation for the rest. Data leaders coming from the business side or even less data-centric technology roles may not have depth or experience in any of the specific DLF disciplines but may be so capable of impacting data value–creating processes that they can accomplish a tremendous amount. By establishing a team around us that can compensate for our own weaknesses, we will be able to bring a complete vision to our companies alongside the abilities to back it up.

The DLF is not a prescriptive tool that will tell us exactly what to do. In fact, on a first read, it probably has us asking more questions than it answers. On subsequent reads, it will do the same thing, and this is exactly the intent.

The path to data value is winding, and nobody can predict exactly what is around the next turn. All we can do is prepare for the challenges we might face.

Balance is key to maximizing the throughput of our data value chain. First, we must evaluate the balance across the five DLF categories, which should always be in relative lockstep with their overall capabilities. To keep the categories in balance, we will deliberately choose which among the twenty DLF disciplines to put energies toward to achieve the most impact with the minimum amount of cost.

As we discussed, the five categories of data leadership are what we are trying to keep in relative balance. Most importantly, we want to balance access, refinement, adoption, and impact. Balancing these is like aligning the sizes of pipes carrying water throughout your home. If you have a big pipe feeding a small pipe feeding another big pipe, the water is not going to flow smoothly. Similar sized pipes will lead to a more efficient flow.

The governance category is more like a pump that pressurizes the water to move it through the pipes. In the data context, this is the momentum of pushing data through the various functions of the data value chain. More literally, it is pushing the simple virtuous cycle to spin as fast as possible!

....

Data leadership is not rocket science. After all, controlled explosions are more predictable than people.

....

The twenty disciplines across the five categories are the machines and controls we use to build the pipes and pump the water through. Unfortunately, unlike the tangible world of water and pipes, these tools are far less precise in how they create data capabilities. This can lead us to unintentional misalignments. Recall the Chris Burke story, where even though we want the categories balanced, our outcomes may vary. Measuring is crucial, because we often won't be able to easily observe the flow of data like the low water pressure in the shower.

With the complexity and nuance of the many facets of data leadership, success won't be easy at first. To be honest, it won't be easy ever! But succeeding with data leadership will be spectacularly worthwhile. And we will get better at it the more we try! In many ways, data leadership is among the most challenging professions an information worker can choose. But when done well, data leadership will completely transform our companies for the better. This adventure makes for a wonderful career, though I'm admittedly biased.

SPEED UP TO SPEED UP

The DLF is, at its best, a useful but incomplete reference architecture to help us navigate our data leadership journeys. We must fill in the details with our unique circumstances, and the priorities are going to vary for every organization too.

....

The DLF strives not to provide the answers but to provide a structured approach in organizing our many questions.

....

Businesses run in countless different ways. Executive leaders have usually spent multiple decades building experience and learning how to be successful in various roles, and they are going to primarily trust what got them to this point. They have built reliable instincts that have served them well.

Data analytics has likely long been part of what these folks do. They have been receiving reports and acting on the insights contained within them for a long time. Occasionally, they will ask for something new or a different kind of detailed break-down, but most requests are built on top of what they already have and are largely rooted in their trusty instincts. At lower levels of an organization, the pattern is similar, but the data has a finer granularity, and the resulting actions are more depart-mental and operations oriented.

....

People at all levels of an organization find that their intuitions are often reinforced by data analytics and vice versa.

....

Data has surrounded us for a long time, and it has been utilized for just as long. What is different today is that our ability to realize value from data is inching forward while the potential value of data is increasing exponentially. By failing to realize a significant percentage of data's potential value, we incur tremendous opportunity costs.

"We have so much to do." "Data challenges are complex." "Coordinating people is hard." "Everybody has a day job." "We are all looking out for number one." "Submit a ticket for that request." "That needs approval." "We can't give you that." "I didn't have time." "Let's have a meeting to discuss." "Sorry, I had a conflict."

Countless reasons (or excuses) exist to slow down or stop. Our corporate default seems to be to delay for anything. What if we could make the standard "go faster unless otherwise proven necessary"?

It is human to want to slow down to get something right first. The thing is, building momentum in data leadership is no different from physics: mass times speed. The faster we move, the more momentum we create. Unless it's clear we'll be able to overwhelmingly recoup later the time we're losing by slowing or standing still now, then we should try to keep making changes that get us moving faster now instead of later. While it is possible to need to slow down to speed up, it is logically much easier to go faster by going faster.

....

If you find yourself suggesting slowing down to speed up, be sure you are right. When in doubt, speed up to speed up.

....

Another common pitfall is to try too hard to hold on to what has been achieved at the expense of what is possible if we keep up our momentum. Look at sports, where the rules and options for success are more limited than in business, resulting in outcomes where winners and losers are clearly identified. How often does the winning team move slower or less decisively than the loser? Reckless decisions are severely punished or rewarded, but a recipe for disaster in any sport is playing "not to lose." Why would our companies, or our data efforts, be any different?

Creating success will be challenging even under the best circumstances, but we will never be successful if we fail to act. Data leadership is about pushing through to data value no matter the obstacles we face.

And even data use isn't enough. In addition to neglecting good data, we are surrounded by spurious data use. Data seems to be misused at least as often as it is productively used. How many organizations out there claim to be *data driven* when they do whatever they want, then look back at carefully selected data and say, "See! The data supports it!" This is not being data driven at all! This is being *data justified*. And how much data value is created when there is no change being driven? That's right: none!

Watch out for the slacker sibling of data *driven*: data *justified*. This is when first a decision is made or activity conducted, and then data is found to support it. So, so wrong!

To do it right, it all comes back to data value. If we are using data to create real differentials in business outcomes, then hopefully we are on the right track. Can data be used to manip-ulate the perceived impacts or show positive net gains when the reality is far worse? Of course. There's also data that, if analyzed properly, will help us uncover any misleading conclusions.

GUT INSTINCTS ARE A REACTION, NOT A DATA REPLACEMENT

I once did some consulting work for an insurance broker. This is the kind of company that does not directly carry risk but instead helps connect people who need insurance with the people who provide insurance. They had many lines of business that grew from that, but they all had a similar pattern of provid-ing business-to-business services related to insurance.

Like many financial services organizations, numbers were everywhere. They were swimming in data, and they had significant challenges trying to manage it all, which I and my colleagues were helping them do. But this is not the point of the story.

The most striking memory I have of that client is that despite its business being fundamentally ruled by analytics, with seriously sophisticated underwriting and risk manage-ment capabilities, as we moved higher in the organization, the numbers seemed to become less important. It was as if higher-level decision-making justified a lack of data analytics rigor.

They managed this large company by the proverbial "gut instinct."

Of course, they received plenty of reports, which they did not trust. They paid lip service to the idea of data governance, but the one executive who spearheaded the whole effort could not muster the broad support necessary to get widespread adoption. At the end of the day, the executives were old-school insurance brokers, focused on their relationships and how things felt instead of what the data was telling them. Though this company continued to perform fine, they will never know where they could be right now if they had maximized their data value.

....

There is no good reason to ignore data analytics that already exist. If you are already on a good path, it can only help.

....

What business leaders need is a better ability to integrate data analytics with their "proven" intuition. Ideally, for the leader, their intuition-based decisions will demonstrate their brilliance, and even the worst-case scenario is that a more rigorous data-centric approach will refine their instincts and actions to drive the best overall business outcomes. This is data leadership at its finest!

The initial push is crucial, because without it, we don't get started at all. Nearly as important but receiving far less attention is the second push, and the one after that, and the one after that...

Sustaining efforts and building momentum over time require the right combination of appropriate targets, virtuous cycles, and folks with motivating incentives. This is table-stakes stuff, regardless of the makeup of the actual team. But there are also patterns of what that team should start to look like as we reach the second push and beyond.

What we will need, regardless of where they come from, is a collective band of folks who together have these powers:

- *Senior Leadership/Executive Visibility:* Able to reach top decision-makers for organizational support and resources.
- *Business Strategy:* Able to understand organizational vision so that potential business outcome differentials align with strategic objectives.
- *Marketing/Sales:* Able to generate support for implementing potential business outcome differentials.
- *Business Process/Operations:* Know the detailed workings of the organization so that potential business outcome differentials are feasible and implementable.
- *Data Analysis:* Able to turn raw data into meaningful insights that will create business outcome differentials.
- *Technology/Database:* Can prepare data via technology systems so that analysis can be performed.

The above items are not ordered by importance but loosely grouped in such a way that if we have three people on our data team, for example, it will be more likely that one person does the first two, the second the next two, etc. But remember, just as every organization is a little bit different, so are data teams and the skills of the individuals within them. We will need to adjust accordingly!

BUILDING AN ALL-STAR DATA LEADERSHIP TEAM

While we data leaders can make a lot happen on our own, we will inevitably need help. Like the more functional skills that we have spent so much time talking about, leadership help can also take many different forms. Before we start our search for more data leaders, it is important to determine what our "asks" of them will be. Useful leadership help tends to be busy, so we are going to need to be prepared to make a strong pitch.

The most *common* ask is for resources (i.e., money and people's time) to help get our data initiatives off the ground. The most *important* ask is to get help engaging with people throughout the organization to understand why data is so important and valuable to the firm and how what we are doing addresses it.

This presumes, of course, that we have already identified something to do that is important and valuable to the firm. If we have not yet reached that point, the efforts in reaching out to other folks will need to take a more inquisitive approach.

Instead of prescribing what others' roles will be, we will look to them for insights on what they and others could do differently if they had more capable data analytics.

There is a difference between asking what someone would do differently and simply asking what kind of data capabilities they want. Data value requires a change in outcomes, driven by a change in decisions or activities, so we need to be direct and deliberate when we create something in the hopes of creating data value.

The senior leadership help we get in defining the mission may not be the same as what will help us most in getting there. Executive vice presidents can be excellent guides on the capabilities that will be most beneficial throughout the organization, but they operate at such an abstracted level of detail that beyond a supportive email or statement, they can only help so much.

When getting an organization's data efforts off the ground, director-level folks are golden. They have connections to the executive suite but still have operational responsibilities and direct reports who tend to be experts in their specific areas.

In a large organization in the early days of data leadership, focus on directors and their direct reports to build the critical mass needed to get off the ground.

This is not to say others at higher and lower levels are unimportant to the success of data leadership. They are certainly important, just less so in the earliest days when most of the organization is blissfully unaware of how much data analytics will change everything.

One less-than-obvious place to find help with data efforts is in the marketing organization. Marketing folks are an incredible untapped data resource in many enterprise data efforts. These people are often already doing more with data and analytics than almost anyone in our companies, and they understand ambiguity and how to use information with imperfect quality. Marketers can also be a bit isolated from the real workings of the business, so getting them more directly involved with creating data value can benefit them in their day jobs as well.

> **If we are fortunate enough to have a marketing department, we should find some way to engage their talent in our data leadership efforts.**

This brings up the biggest obstacle standing in the way of maximizing data value: managing organizational change. People are generally change averse, and even once you manage to break down the walls of initial resistance, there is only so much change the people of an organization can handle at once. Data people tend to get all excited about everything they can do to change things for the better, and it ends up overwhelming *everybody else.*

It's helpful to think of *everybody else* as potential clients for our data efforts. These folks do not owe us data leaders anything. They have jobs to do, and it is up to us to show them that we can help improve their lives. This assumes that we have a realistically executable plan on how to improve their lives.

> **Be prepared to do marketing and sales for data efforts, and do not expect an if-we-build-it-they-will-come approach to be enough.**

The people on the front lines of our organizations are often the closest to our external customers and to the data we talk so much about. Business operations are where much of our data is born, and the folks creating it probably know more about it than anybody else. If we ever hope to establish better data quality, for example, that path runs right through operations. So why not get them involved early? This could take the form of asking them to complete surveys or even giving them a spot on our core data team.

There is a TV show that became popular in recent years called *Undercover Boss*. The premise is that company CEOs pretend to be junior employees, and hilarity ensues. The "boss" is usually embarrassingly bad at the lower-level job and then learns an important lesson in the end. There are usually hugs, and crying is often involved. It's all quite formulaic. But why is it such a popular show? It's because people are so desperate to be heard by leadership that they will spend their free time watching a show that gives them a glimpse of what that might be like. Also, it's good entertainment to watch silly executives fail at basic tasks and then get all emotional about it.

This further highlights a common disconnect between management and what is really happening in their businesses. I've always been a bit in awe of those CEOs who work their way up from the mail room (or comparable low-level job) and after thirty years make it to the top. To have that kind of tenacity and dedication is a quality we just do not see enough of anymore. Hopefully, these leaders do not forget where they came from and continue to remember what it was like on the front lines.

For those of us who change jobs more frequently, we will not usually have the direct experience that perfectly overlaps with our operational folks, and to be fair, even the homegrown CEO didn't personally hold every job in the organization. We must try to directly elicit as much information as possible, and the rest of the time, we must rely on our own personal experience as a proxy, trying to relate these to many more situations than those we've had ourselves.

One experience I often look back on was when I was working at a country club halfway house the summer after my freshman year of college. The halfway house was where we made snacks and sandwiches for golfers who were halfway through their eighteen-hole round, not to be confused with a halfway house that helps ease the transition between prison and freedom.

One golfer who had ordered a hot dog, after signing his slip to pay, asked me if I had touched his hot dog. I explained that yes, I did touch his food long enough to wrap it up. He then, without another word, threw out the hot dog and left. The thought that a kitchen worker may have touched his food was enough to get him to play nine more holes of golf without the nourishment he needed for top performance, though the six beers he also purchased would hopefully keep him properly hydrated.

Recall the earlier discussion around empowerment and accountability? My country club hot dog story is an example of holding someone accountable without corresponding empowerment. At the end of it, one person had spent some money and left dissatisfied with the value he received, and the other got an anecdote for a book someday. Wouldn't it be an amazing twist if the golfer was *actually* Chris Burke from my earlier baseball story? It wasn't, but in the movie adaptation, we'll make it happen!

Anyway, I learned at that pivotal lunchtime moment that some people have unreasonable expectations, and sometimes there will be nothing we can do to fix them. I also learned that some people will always think they are better than others, and I resolved never to be one of those people.

> **Everybody has something to teach us. As much as we might know ourselves, there will be another person with a deeper understanding or a specialized perspective that gives new insights on the topic.**

In the early days of our data leadership journey, we must find help from those who can identify the truths that we will need to understand to drive data value. Wonder why data scientists are such a hot commodity these days? They are seen as the oracles that can lead us from data chaos to data value. One person can do with data the equivalent of taking raw carbon and turning it into a perfectly cut diamond ring—impressive!

The downside is that this is not a particularly scalable process. We hear data scientists referred to as "unicorns," and whether that is an apt description is debatable. But what is not debatable is the fact that if we want to operationalize data scientists' outcomes (effectively creating diamonds from raw carbon), we are not going to be able to staff the data mines with a herd of unicorns. If we're lucky enough to have any high-performing data scientists in our midst, we must focus on amplifying their artisanal capabilities through operational integration.

> **We must build the operational ability to transform data science prototypes into functioning data value systems that will serve our businesses' needs at scale.**

The worst thing we can do is ask the data scientists to transform their big ideas into operational realities themselves. It would be like asking a shoe cobbler to run Nike's factories and sales channels. The skill sets required are mostly divergent, though there will certainly be places where the cobbler's expert knowledge and advice would help inform the design of the scaled-up processes and systems.

To appropriately lead the charge to improve an organization's data-driven abilities, we need a data leader who can communicate with the data scientists, the broader technology teams, the business executives, all departments, and the frontline workers and who knows a lot about data management, governance, and the whole data world. We might just need a chief data officer!

13

LEADING DATA LEADERSHIP

DATA LEADERSHIP IS BUSINESS LEADERSHIP
We have devoted a lot of time to exploring the kinds of change and outcomes we are looking to drive in the pursuit of data value for our organizations. The perspective has been one of a general leader floating somewhere in the orbit of data, technology, and business management responsibilities. This is intentional, as data leadership is foundational and can be driven from anywhere in the organization.

Especially as data leadership efforts get off the ground and evolve into more pervasive capabilities intertwined with the entire business, we need to address how to provide the right leadership roles to scale data leadership to its full potential. As we have also noted, our current organizational structures are not doing particularly well at leading existing change or operations functions that stretch across all our business units.

Every organization is different, with distinct leadership and reporting lines that may reflect industry norms and needs, ownership structures, and even size or age. There's no point in covering them in detail here, but there are three key roles that are commonly misunderstood, misused, or missed entirely. These are the chief data officer (CDO), chief information officer (CIO), and consultants. All three can be instrumental in creating data value, and all (or the lack thereof) have the potential to destroy the best efforts of the rest of our data leaders.

We'll start with the least known and most missed (CDO), progress through the better known and equally misunderstood (CIO), and end with the most misused and least missed (consultants). Though we can't resist a good joke at the expense of consultants, do not let this diminish the role they have to play. After all, you may not be able to get your board to greenlight a CDO right now, but if you are serious about data value, you may need to rely on some external help in the meantime.

Seeing as how we're coming perilously close to giving consultants a proper compliment, we'd better get back on track with the CDO. Your business really needs one of these.

THE CHIEF DATA OFFICER

CDO is a title that has enjoyed increasing popularity in the business community generally but especially in data management and data governance circles. Data folks seem to interpret this as a coming-out party for what we do, but it may speak just as loudly to the fact that people recognize there is a problem but still haven't agreed on an approach to solve it.

Note that some organizations choose to call this new role a chief analytics officer (CAO) or chief digital officer (also CDO). Some of the detailed responsibilities vary with the emphasis connoted by the title, but the gist of the role is effectively the same: maximizing data value creation at an organizational level. For our purposes, we're going to use CDO as the catchall for these titles.

A CDO maximizes data value creation throughout the entire organization.

The role and level of the CDO varies widely from organization to organization. Many so-called CDOs have no direct reports. How is someone with no people on their team going to be a chief of anything? This sounds like someone with a role without a proper balance between empowerment and accountability. If people filling these CDO roles are willing to accept impossible jobs, then it hurts the entire community.

We must balance pragmatism with our need to work with what we have. If they want to call us CDO but not give us the tools to do that job, we must insist on something more appropriate for right now, like "data leadership advocate." That way, we have a title that reflects our responsibility (empowerment and accountability), and after we knock that out of the park, we will have room for title growth as our team and scope of influence continue to expand.

We need something that looks like a CDO—someone whose job it is to tirelessly maximize data value for an organization by overseeing the many data management–related activities that must work in tandem. This is less about the specific title and more about how to fulfill these vast responsibilities within the context of a complex organization.

Data people love to have the same conversation repeatedly. Attend a data conference and we are inevitably confronted with questions like "What skills are necessary to be a good CDO?" and "Where should the CDO report in an organization?"

It's as if the CDO were some sort of data superhero. Where do these mysterious beings come from? Do CDOs come from project management, technical teams, or a planet in a neighboring galaxy? Do their mythical powers derive from magic or a terrible science experiment?

We want our CDOs to be knowledgeable executives, accomplished managers, profound business minds, and brilliant technologists. Yes, that sounds fantastic! In the real world, we have individuals, all of whom have unique career stories. They have strengths, weaknesses, and résumé gaps. We can talk of ideals, but we must hire real people who will never quite fit perfectly.

....

A good CDO candidate will be able to help our businesses use data to get better at what they do. Find the best person at doing that, and where they came from will be less important than where they will help us go.

....

Let's assume we have a CDO candidate identified. This is often a new position in the organization, whose responsibilities are clearly important but cross over many functions that we already have in our businesses. It is often a nontrivial exercise to figure out how to fit the role in organizationally.

An early question we must ask our organizations is whether CDOs should report to IT or the business. A common response among data professionals is, "Of course the CDO should report to the business! Don't be silly! The data is too important to be left to IT's crazy ways!"

This kind of groupthink reaction is not only scary, but it fails to fully consider the résumé requirements of being a CDO alongside the empowerment and accountability balance that they will need to successfully perform their role. Let's break it down a little more carefully:

- **Does data need technology to be made useful? (Yes.)**
- **Does IT do technology stuff for your company? (Yes.)**
- **Does the business rely on IT to support other essential business functions? (Yes.)**
- **Therefore, the CDO should obviously report to the business and not IT. (???)**

Why are we even having this conversation? IT is overwhelmingly the most logical place for the CDO to reside.

This is a bold statement. It may even elicit a visceral negative response inside those of us who know for a fact if we put the role of the CDO inside IT, the CDO will be less effective in our organizations. Why is that? Have we completely lost faith in our technology people to be a trusted part of the business?

Well, in a word, yes.

....

Any debate about the CDO reporting to anywhere other than IT is because IT has lost its relevance to the business.

....

Our technology organizations have been failing our businesses for a long time. This failure is embedded in the culture and language of IT operations. For example, "requirements gathering" connotes a unidirectional flow of information from the business to IT. It's like a Taco Bell drive-through: "I'll have the Office 365 burrito please, and 2 ERP soft tacos." Coming right up! What kind of sauce would you like?

IT has been trained to focus their energy on assembling outputs from their core ingredients on request. They get talked at by the business and then do whatever is necessary to keep from being yelled at. Not being yelled at is a surprisingly good motivator.

When IT becomes overwhelmed with requests, things slow down, and eventually they start to say no. Relations between the business and IT degrade, shadow IT pops up, and everybody is angry with each other. Something big must be done.

Enter the CDO. Here is a technology-ish person who cares! Somebody who "gets" the business and has empathy for their needs. Certainly, the CDO will be a real partner who will get it right this time, even though they are often given a minuscule team with a vague mandate and no real authority beyond that. What could go wrong?

We are watching history repeat itself. We've been down this road before. The CIO role was created decades ago for this exact reason! The chief technology officers (CTOs) of the world became too focused with the internal departmental challenges of producing and operating capable technology solutions on behalf of their businesses. The CTOs underinvested in their business strategy and alignment responsibilities because those outputs were harder to measure and probably seemed less important than the technical challenges of running IT. Or maybe they were simply trying to get people to stop yelling at them.

Over time, it became clear that, in many organizations, IT had lost its way by seemingly focusing on things that the business couldn't care less about. To restore the business-first focus of the IT department, the CIO role was created to oversee all organizational information assets without being operationally responsible for all the technology. What happened is that over time, the CIOs underinvested in their business strategy and alignment responsibilities and have become too focused on the day-to-day operations of technology development and support.

And today the cycle repeats, but instead of putting the CDO as the head of the IT group, they are being put in other business units, entirely removed from oversight of the technology systems necessary to achieve data value. This is treating symptoms without addressing the real underlying problems, and it is not going to solve the organizational challenges we've always faced. To break the cycle, we are going to need to fix the real problem. This is the real reason why we put CIO second in this list: it's their fault we are in this mess.

THE CHIEF INFORMATION OFFICER

CIOs need to be actual C-level executives. This means a strategic business function with a meaningful impact to the success of the company. By necessity, it is a role with a profit-and-loss responsibility. Success at the C-level requires a measurable contribution, and that must be a balanced one. The head of a cost center cannot be an effective C-level executive.

Organizations need to evaluate why CIOs are not living up to their expectations instead of creating new C-level positions set up to fail in new ways.

But creating poor positions is not the only problem. An even bigger challenge is that we have few truly qualified candidates to fill these roles, whether we call them CIOs or CDOs. Remember, the current engagement model of our technology organizations is that of manning takeout windows: gathering requirements and delivering projects with no expectation of creativity or problem solving beyond technical specifications. This has led to a world where we have few strategically aligned technology professionals available to perform true business executive CIO roles.

Despite this, CIOs are everywhere. Most are performing incomplete functions with incomplete skills, delivering incomplete value. We must stop filling our CIO positions with technology directors or CTO equivalents. Our CDOs aren't real C-level positions unless they are in lieu of a CIO, and our data systems builders should absolutely report up to the CDO, if they exist.

A CDO's domain of responsibility is a subset of the CIO's, not a separate one. But when the CIO is a technology operations person with the wrong title, this relationship becomes less obvious.

What we need are better CIOs. We need people who are asked to be strategic parts of the business from early in their careers, not just when they reach the top and wonder why they don't really have a seat at the table. We need to completely rethink the role of technology and data throughout our organizations. These are good ideas, but they are also big, sweeping changes that we will need years to achieve. What can be done now?

First, we must learn from within. Data systems development and operations have not yet embraced the collaborative techniques the applications side of technology has created. Agile, DevOps, continuous testing/deployment, NoSQL, cloud technologies—all these can begin to help us understand how to react more nimbly. These are technology-driven innovations that we can build on from within our IT and data groups. The greater challenge is rebuilding a healthy relationship between IT and the business. This is where there is no secret formula.

....

Building IT into a critical business capability requires executive sponsorship, strong leadership throughout, and a good amount of empathy.

....

We need to want to unite to make our organizations better. In the end, we should stop caring so much about the CDO. We shouldn't pretend that this singular position fundamentally changes anything by itself. We must address the real problems that cause our organizations to break down.

Let's find ways to drive business innovation with data. Invest in that however we can, in any way it works for our business. Our competitors are certainly doing the same. Our customers will tell us the path we must take to be successful. We should listen to them. Adjust. Improve. Listen some more. Where have we seen that pattern before?

CONSIDERING CONSULTANTS

Thinking about the many different roles and functions we need internally can become overwhelming. We may feel alone and confused. Fear not, as there are plenty of folks out there who would like to help us. They are consultants, and they can let us tap into a wealth of experience and skills that can be difficult to obtain from within our organizations.

Consultants spend a lot of time and energy becoming and staying knowledgeable in their areas of expertise. Well, good ones do at least. Mediocre consultants focus less on building their own capabilities and more on convincing whomever they can that they are knowledgeable. Watch out for those who claim to know it all but cannot back it up. The consultants who go to great lengths to show you how smart they are will tend to let you down when the stakes are highest.

....

Data leadership as a subject is so broad that it's essential to get help in specific disciplines or with general analysis and strategy.

....

The wisest among us recognize how little they know compared to the sum of the folks around them. As we learn more and realize how much bigger data leadership is than we originally thought, it is reasonable to want some help with it. This is exactly why consultants exist and why they can help us—if we know how to use them.

Consultants have a binary existence. They are either *billing*, or charging clients for services, which makes everybody happy because it brings in dollars to keep the consulting firm running, or they are *not billing*, which means they are using that time to learn new tricks and trying desperately to get back to billing before they get fired or the business folds. It can be a painfully cyclical process, far removed from the cliché images portrayed by TV shows like *House of Lies*.

It is important to think about the consulting business model to understand the incentives that motivate consultants. If we understand their motivations, then we will be able to appropriately assess our interactions with them and evaluate the worthwhileness of proposed engagements.

Consultants want to be billable, and consulting firms want to have their people be as billable as possible—this is how the money gets made. It's a reasonable business model, but it causes some inherent conflicts of interest related to serving clients effectively.

When a consultant's help is no longer required, their desire to remain billable may conflict with the client's needs.

Ask any consultant about the importance of "follow-on work" (a.k.a. "after work"). This is the foundation of the traditional consulting business model—an initial strategy engagement followed by years of full-time implementation work by a couple dozen lower-level associates raking in higher-level fees! Greed is good! Money, money, money!

This model is disgusting. Nowhere in there is even a thought about what the client needs. Consultants who make it all about themselves may find ways to make a lot of money, but they will never earn it.

Greed driven consultants have never seen a potential client that doesn't desperately need what they are selling. To paraphrase the old saying, if you are selling *hammers*, everything is a *nail*!

Given the broad scope of data leadership, every organization may need some additional help, but the path forward does not *require* consultants. The catch is that without consultants, there is an enormous amount of learning and experience we still need to find somewhere—either by growing it internally or hiring folks with those skills (who would otherwise likely be consultants themselves). Regardless, some amount of investment will be required, and most organizations will find that occasionally bringing in some help from consultants will be the best way to get the extra capabilities we need.

An approach some organizations use to find external help is the request for proposal (RFP). This is where the client organization creates a typically lengthy document that outlines everything they would like to see in an upcoming project. Consulting firms then bid on the project or pieces of the project, and the client organization reviews and selects the proposal and firm they like best.

RFPs are particularly common in the public sector and with large companies that are going to be spending lots of money on an upcoming project. These RFPs take a significant amount of effort to write on the client side and a significant amount of work on the consulting firm side to respond—and with a relatively small chance for any individual consulting firm to win the work.

This leads to some unintended consequences. In most RFPs, the selection criteria are dominated by pricing, typically alongside a check-the-box assessment of whether the proposal satisfies the particular requirements of the RFP. This leads to the lowest-cost provider having a built-in advantage over more capable but more costly proposals.

Consulting firms with higher service quality levels tend to perform worse in RFPs because these firms are less likely to cut corners to reduce costs and therefore less likely to win bids systemically biased toward the lowest-cost solutions.

Additionally, there is a phenomenon in any bidding scenario known as the "winner's curse." This means that whichever firm bids the lowest is the most likely to have made a significant mistake in estimating the resources they will need to complete the project successfully. Because they were willing to quote the lowest price, the firm must have some combination of a willingness to accept lower margins, a more efficient delivery model, or a differing assessment of the project itself.

This implies that the firm most likely to win an RFP by virtue of low pricing will probably end up losing money on the project. Unless, of course, the consultant finds ways to cut corners in delivery or add scope (and cost) to the total project. Sadly, some firms specialize in doing just this. They will under-bid the project to win it and then rely on change requests and additional fees to make their money. This creates an environment where the best consulting firms will often avoid RFPs altogether because of the low likelihood of them being a good ROI in the end.

These are risks and trade-offs that arise with RFPs, but they can be mitigated. If we are in an organization setting up and evaluating RFPs, we should try to base the selection criteria on a more balanced value concept rather than incomplete pricing criteria. Instead of passively posting the RFP on a website where people need to hunt it down, let's identify several known high-quality firms and actively invite them to create a proposal. And the easier it is for the consulting firms to participate, the more qualified responses we'll get.

Finally, we should establish reasonable ways to handle new information that arises during the project or may not have been completely explained in the original RFP. Incentivize vendor performance to encourage delivery excellence. And remember, though it is perfectly laudable to seek good value, we will inevitably get what we pay for.

....

We should not try to take advantage of our consulting partners, and then we will be justified in demanding they do not try to take advantage of us.

....

Regardless of how the consulting selection process happens, whenever we choose to use consultants, there are some actions we can take to encourage the most productive outcomes.

First, if the proposal is for a strategy project that includes an assessment and corresponding recommendations, we should be extra careful. Most consultant recommendations will include follow-on work for that firm, with varying levels of justification. We must insist that consultants make recommendations that are not predicated on their continued involvement. It is fine to have the option to continue with the consultant's help, but we must also have a viable path forward without them.

Second, if the deliverables are something like a PowerPoint

deck and executive read-out presentation, we are in danger of the deliverables becoming "shelfware." This is when a well-intentioned consulting project was completed, but there were no additional resources available for the recommended follow-on implementation efforts. The deliverables become stale over time, and when the client organization is ready to move forward, they need to do another strategic assessment to understand how things have changed since the last one. Organizations have done this multiple times without ever getting to the real work of fixing things! The way to mitigate shelfware is to first line up more resources than just what is required by the assessment, and we should be committed to act regardless of how scary the recommendations turn out to be. Let's gain agreement on an ongoing engagement model with any external entities from the very beginning. It can benefit everyone to move away from a project/transactional relationship to one with a deeper commitment to long-term improvements and one where the real business impacts (good or bad) are shared with the consulting partners who helped create them. This will only work if there is trust between client and consultant, and that takes time too.

This is a demanding approach and one that may chase away those firms that have solved for the price-biased RFP approach. The consultants who remain may be expensive, because it is not easy to become good enough to sign up for this kind of arrangement. These consultants also tend to be busy, as they tend to have many clients that will never let them go. These are the kind of partners we want alongside us on our data value journey.

....

As important and central as people are to data success, it would be wrong to think that technology is less important. It's really about balance, just like so much of what we've covered so far.

....

In the DLF, we've discussed how new technologies may capture people's attention, and we will need to acknowledge that if we want to gain support for our essential but perhaps less-inspirational endeavors. Because many of us have limited opportunities to learn about the tools and technologies our companies have not yet adopted, the next chapter provides some background and basic information on the latest new technologies with which all data leaders should have some familiarity.

14

DATA LEADERSHIP TECHNOLOGIES TO KNOW

STRONG LEADERSHIP GETS MORE DONE WITH POWERFUL TOOLS

Data without technology is like space flight without technology: we won't be getting very far. Technology evolves quickly and has reached the point where nobody can keep track of all the latest trends or understand everything that might be useful to our organizations.

....

Data leaders are probably the best-equipped folks to understand enough of both the business and technical sides of the technology innovation equation, and if we don't put it all together, who will?

....

Thinking about new technology solutions is a risky proposition, because without discipline, we can fall into the trap of becoming too product focused. Technology at its best is a pure amplifier of everything else we have talked about in this book—it does not solve our problems for us. At its worst, technology adds so much noise and inefficiency to our data efforts that it sabotages everything we might attempt to do. If we keep this power versus risk dynamic in mind as we walk this virtual showcase, we should be okay.

There are shiny objects that can easily distract our team members if we are not careful. Depending on our perspective, the good news or bad news is that technologies are a heck of a lot of fun for us data leaders too! Who wouldn't want to play with the tech that is in the news and capturing everybody's imagination?

Tech is like candy to data leaders. We want it, and it tastes good when we get it. It may even give us a nice boost of energy for a little while! But then, once the sugar rush wears off, we regret blowing our diet on it. It's not that the latest technologies are bad; it's just that they are not as nutritious to our organizations as more fundamental improvements to data capabilities.

We really should eat our vegetables before we have dessert. This is *not* the place to start, except when it is. This means that people are going to want fancy-pants technologies, even when they do not have basic reporting or core access and refinement capabilities. Just like most kids don't know why they should eat their spinach before indulging in the KitKats, our data consumers don't know why they shouldn't have real-time streaming before they can balance the financial statements.

This presents us with somewhat of an ethical dilemma. As you now know from reading this far, we would probably be encouraging suboptimal resource investments if we let folks jump straight to tech before getting the basics right. However, if we refuse to give them what they are asking for, they will simply replace us with someone else who will, and our replacement will likely not even know the path of pain they are heading down. This also seems less than ideal.

The answer is a balanced solution that parents will find familiar: let them have a little candy if they eat their vegetables too. We give them some cutting-edge tech to keep their interest while also allocating enough resources to accomplish our core objectives.

This keeps the business sponsors interested and gives us a chance to give them something that will help in the end. This pattern happens more frequently than we would like. People have become conditioned to buy products and "quick fix" solutions rather than addressing the underlying problems.

If we fail to excel at basic data capabilities, the advanced stuff will only amplify our problems.

Data is too close to the core of an organization to be solved by a single product, no matter how amazing it is (even if Apple made it!). At this point, we understand that data is every one of our businesses, and we data leaders must be the masters of our own destiny. Technologies give us the power to create data value at scale, and as data leaders, we will find ourselves involved in discussions about technologies in which our organizations might invest.

While technologies, especially new and emerging

technologies, are exciting and get all our hope juices flowing, it is critically important to recognize that they represent only a small part of most organizations' data value chains. At the same time, if we don't dream big, we are unlikely to get very far.

As we've mentioned before, the goal is to introduce a few things worth researching further; these descriptions are short, subjective opinions that do not provide a particularly balanced view. Is that disclaimered enough for you?

IN-MEMORY

This is as good a place as any to start. Tableau raised the bar for interactive dashboards and visualizations with its in-memory technology, so much so that now that's what people often think about when they think of business intelligence tools. It's almost like Kleenex for data! Though the interactive and graphical capabilities are compelling, it's Tableau's ability to process data files and store them in memory that allows users to do interactive business intelligence without an underlying database. It may be common now, but it is still very cool. Other tools have expanded on Tableau's power in the data processing space and, with today's computing power, have put a staggering amount of data analytics power in the hands of a single analyst.

GRAPH DATABASES

These are data repositories structured to understand the relationships between data. They facilitate smarter search capabilities where you do not have to guess the keyword precisely, which is bafflingly how many search tools still work. Search today is still riddled with text-based, hunt-and-peck embarrassments. And don't get me started on SharePoint!

Amazon's Alexa is slightly better than the legacy search tools because at least she helps us shop for stuff we don't need. In more successful use cases, graph database capabilities are transforming industries like pharmaceutical research, document management, and legal discovery. With knowledge graphs on the back end, coupled with machine learning and AI (refer back to the Data Science DLF discipline for more on these), human lawyers will be able to produce results at a much faster pace, which should eventually make legal services more cost effective.

NOSQL

This is hardly an emerging technology, but there are plenty of companies (and data professionals!) that still have not yet embraced the power of NoSQL. This is equally unsurprising and unacceptable. NoSQL is a technology that stores data in one of two forms: document or key-value pairs, the differences of which are less important right now than knowing those terms generally relate to NoSQL. This technology is particularly useful for quick retrieval of a specific data record that contains metadata about the referenced item. Websites work this way, with IDs that are sent to the web server, then used to query a NoSQL database to locate all the information about our accounts. NoSQL does not do a very good job at aggregating information. If we are doing a lot of math, we're better off sticking with a relational database variant.

GRAPHICAL INFORMATION SYSTEMS

GIS is completely taken for granted by us in our personal lives, but once learning how it works, it is mind-blowing. Our GPS systems rely on a precise understanding of latitude and longitude along with ultraprecise clocks. Oversimplified, a location is found by comparing the slight time differences received from multiple satellites and then triangulating from those differences. The underlying database of addresses, roads, and terrain, composed of points and lines, is possible thanks to GIS. GPS systems are not the only use case for GIS—if we care about looking at anything through space and time, we care about GIS. When we think about what is on the horizon with IoT, GIS is going to only get more important.

CLOUD

For anybody who has studied even basic economics, the benefits of the cloud should be fairly evident. The cloud involves sharing computing infrastructure investments across many organizations that do not drive their competitive advantage through unique hardware. For most organizations, if technology is a competitive differentiator, it is going to be through the software layer. This implies that procuring commodity hardware with economies of scale is an optimal approach. Through the network effects of having many purchasers with differing consumption patterns, cloud technology providers like Amazon Web Services can create new computing consumption models never possible with on-premises infrastructure. We will talk more about the cloud later, but the power and economies are so compelling that any organization not moving in that direction is becoming an ostrich (i.e., putting its head in the sand, unwilling to see the danger in its current situation).

SERVERLESS

Serverless runtime containers are at the logical limit of cloud infrastructure innovation. It used to be that we would have to manually instantiate a server instance to then run our code, but that either took significant ramp-up and ramp-down cycles, or we still had underutilized servers sitting around. Instead of provisioning a functional machine or virtual machine, why bother with machine instantiation overhead at all? Cloud providers have now enabled runtime containers that allow us to execute code and simply pay for the computing power actually consumed. They simplify developers' lives and provide a near-perfect elasticity between utilization and costs.

INTERNET OF THINGS

The dream of the Twitter-enabled refrigerator is not what to think about with IoT. Instead, think about the smart watches that track your steps, sleep, and heart rate and then allow you to visualize and track your health goals. Think about air qual ity sensors that enable text messaging if your allergy trigger is high today. Think about the manufacturing sensors that will give some of our oldest businesses incredible new insights on how to become more efficient. IoT is not going to have one killer app; it's going to be much more like a swarm of bees. One by itself won't change much, but a few billion will create a lot of honey—or sting a lot of people.

PYTHON/R

Python (and its data science cousin R) merit mentioning because these programming languages have helped drive faster develop-ment processes and play particularly nicely in the cloud and IoT spaces. When I first learned Python, I was amazed. The syntax was straightforward and easy to write, but the biggest benefit came from how easy it is to extend. There is a centralized library where, with a single command, you can download already-written application capabilities to use in your code. This makes programming in Python more like assembling blocks, whereas other common languages require the developer to build up more from scratch. This may not be so impressive to folks who have been deep in the Linux world for a long time, but being unaware of this shared-building-blocks approach is often a blinder for those of us who have been isolated in the Windows or Oracle ecosystems for too long.

BLOCKCHAIN

Many folks are convinced that blockchain will be the next major technology disruptor.[1] A blockchain is effectively an immutable database that, in theory, cannot be corrupted due to its lack of centralized management. Think of open-source software, but instead of code, it's data, and instead of freely sharing the information with everybody, privacy is protected because everything in the blockchain is extra encrypted with no way to reverse engineer without the source key. This secrecy-in-plain-sight approach enables cryptocurrencies, which have had a wild ride lately, but this is just the most well-known application of blockchain. The implications for health care, like electronic medical records that are perfectly up-to-date no matter which provider you visit, would potentially transform that industry. Every industry may have a similarly compelling use case, but only time will tell.

BIG DATA

For the last approximately fifty years, we have had different ways of storing, accessing, and aggregating data in databases and other mechanisms. Big data represented the size, speed, or complexity of data beyond what the current systems at any time could reasonably handle. It was a constantly moving target, making it a lousy point of reference.

We have now reached a point where we can scale without an effective limit. Terabytes, *please*—child's play! Petabytes, no problem. Even exabytes can be handled with today's systems. Need to look up how big an exabyte is? Quick answer, it is more than you have. A slightly longer answer based on what I found in Wikipedia is that an exabyte is approximately fifteen thousand times more information than the words in all the books ever written, including this one. It's a million terabytes. It is unbelievably big, *big data*.

The conversation about big data is now over: we can handle anything. Any amount of data we can possibly obtain can be elegantly managed by today's data systems. It may be expensive, but it absolutely can be done.

PUBLIC CLOUD: AN ENTIRE CLASS OF TECHNOLOGIES

The single most important factor contributing to the exponential growth in our ability to handle very large data sets is the decoupling of access to computing power from the need to manage physical infrastructure. In simpler terms, the advent of the public cloud.

Big, smart companies realized years ago that they could operate large data centers with better economies of scale than individual companies, and if they created an effective interface into the resulting computing capabilities, other companies would be willing to pay for it. This was established at Amazon Web Services from the early days of their retail organization, when Amazon was built using these same frameworks. Exciting times for a burgeoning business when starting with a marquee client from day one and that client is also you! As prescient as that original idea was, nobody could fully imagine the kinds of dynamic new technologies and design patterns that would grow from those early days.

Today the cloud offers the ability to scale processing down to responding to individual microevents, with à la carte pricing available down to fractions of a second! Buying that ETL server that sits idle for eighteen hours a day maybe seems a bit suboptimal now, doesn't it?

Here are five reasons to consider embracing a cloud-first strategy.

INSTANT INFRASTRUCTURE AVAILABILITY

Anyone who has built technology systems for any amount of time has had this happen. Our project finally gets the green light from the business, the finance people, and anybody else who likes to say no, and what happens?

We wait.

Well, first we go through the hassles of ordering the new data center equipment, and then we wait for it to be processed, shipped, installed, configured, and provisioned, and then we might be able to start working with it. Typically, it takes weeks if not months of hassle and delay.

In the cloud, the high-level process is roughly the same, except the steps all happen through a console on our PC, and it takes about five minutes from start to finish.

And that's for planned infrastructure availability. Unplanned infrastructure availability takes the same amount of time once we have made the decision to do it. We'll want to have some internal controls in place to keep people from going nuts with it, but that's a problem worth solving to cut weeks or months off every acquisition of new computing power.

After all, isn't this how things should be? The hard part should be strategically deciding what to do. Everything else is just friction between the potential value of an opportunity and realizing the value from it. Comparing it to the old ways of procuring infrastructure, the cloud makes traditional data center supply chain delays seem nothing short of ridiculous.

INFINITE SCALABILITY

Speaking of ridiculous, at various points in previous, unenlightened, on-premises stops in my career, I would be building a new database environment and realize I'd need new server on which to run my creation. I'd put together a business case asking for some money, eventually get approval, and then order the equipment.

Inevitably, I'd be contacted by somebody in a deeper, darker IT cave than the one in which I lived, and they would ask me the question I hated most: "So what specs do you need on that server?"

As a database-centric geek, I knew I wanted something good, but I had no idea how my database performance translated into the server specifications. Knowing I'd only have one chance to buy the machine I needed, I wasn't going to err on the side of underpowered or undersized. Naturally, I'd get the biggest, fastest, most expensive option that didn't exceed my budget. And the IT purchaser couldn't have cared less—they just wanted their headache (me) to go away.

The net result is that companies with on-premises data center equipment probably spent more than they needed to on servers, but their databases had plenty of processing headroom. But what was the alternative—accidentally get too weak of a machine? Doom the project before one piece of software is written or applied? No thank you. Gimme the good one!

....

One might argue that the misalignment of excess computing power acquired versus what was necessary is just one more intrinsic cost of living in the old data center world.

....

Now, with the cloud, we can manage infrastructure resources the way we develop code: trial and error. See if it works; if not, make some changes. The scalability of the cloud is so limitless, it enables entirely new ways of working with infrastructure. We can start with our best guess and then iteratively measure performance and change the underlying capabilities on the fly.

This is especially helpful in new environments that may receive little traffic initially but will grow in usage over time. We can even configure environments to scale automatically based on usage metrics that are natively tracked. But the most exciting extension of unlimited scalability is not how big we can grow it but how small!

NEW DEVELOPMENT APPROACHES

Some of the latest innovations in cloud technologies are microservices and serverless computing. Microservice applications typically do a discrete task, like land an individual data file in a database table. Serverless computing essentially allows the resources to exist only if we need to run a small application.

The magic is in how they are instantiated. Sure, we *can* schedule them to run at set times, but that misses the point. The beauty of microservices is that they are designed to be event driven. Cloud service providers have developed mechanisms that watch for specific conditions to occur, like a file being saved to disk, and then fire up the microservice applications that are ready to respond to these conditions. This allows much greater variability in how we process data. ETL should long ago have moved away from rigid processing structures and once-a-day batches.

....

With microservices and serverless computing as a backbone, we can change everything about how we process data and start breaking down the time and complexity barriers that cause delays between data being available and the business being able to act on it.

....

Just think: now we can truly build iteratively with data! As business requirements evolve, so can our technical approach, in tandem with our underlying hardware. In a pay-what-we-use model, we have perfect elasticity in keeping and enhancing what works while discarding the less effective approaches. The bottleneck returns to where it should be, which is the ability of the business to make decisions and the skills of the people who carry out those decisions.

UNPARALLELED POWER

Cloud technologies unlock capabilities that were recently fantasy. An individual business can plug into effectively infinite computing power, changing resource allocations in constant response to its evolving needs.

The most exciting aspect is that we shouldn't need to wait weeks or months to make new analytics capabilities available to the business. Turnaround times can be as short as minutes or hours for tasks that used to take much longer. The power of the cloud enables us to implement fully interactive, data warehouse–driven solutions in the time it once took to deliver a basic report.

To realize the potential of the cloud, we need to adopt new methodologies and train our people to interact differently, as real partners.

Business and technology must solve problems together, iteratively, with the impact to the business always top of mind. Whether we choose to adopt a well-defined agile scrum approach or simply change reporting structures and leave it up to individual managers, we must learn to operate in a new way.

It's like the discovery of nuclear energy. Cloud technologies are that powerful in the data and computational area. As nuclear energy did for submarines, cloud technologies can be harnessed to provide businesses power that fundamentally changes what they can accomplish. Similarly, without proper controls and governance, things can rapidly get out of hand.

These are the kinds of challenges we want in our businesses: all the power we could ever use, with a model that allows us to start small, experiment, and build on top of what works. This leads to the bottom line: a cost-benefit ratio possibly higher than any other investment our businesses could make.

OFF-THE-CHARTS COST-BENEFIT RATIOS

Many organizations have recently adopted a cloud-based, columnar storage/massively parallel processing data warehouse product. This product has all the scalability capabilities of the cloud but can be had for about $1,000 per terabyte per year and starts at about $250 a month all in. It wasn't too long ago that the only way into this kind of technology was a dedicated data center appliance, with a $100,000+ price tag before we'd even turn it on.

Because the technology is so inexpensive at small scale, we can do a pilot project with real data in just a couple of weeks from start to end. When is the last time any data-related project with a measurable business impact was done in two weeks? Most projects can't even be scoped in two weeks! Therein lies the opportunity—and the challenge. What we've glimpsed here scratches the surface of what the cloud is and how it can impact our world of data and analytics.

One downside that must be noted is that with the ease of turning on additional cloud resources, it can lead to sprawl and out of control costs. This is not a fault of cloud technologies themselves, but the processes organizations have in place to manage their use. Some companies err on the side of locking the cloud down too much and removing many of the benefits. Others quickly find themselves with huge bills with no understanding of what the resources are being used for, or the value being created as a result. None of these are good reasons to avoid cloud, but are good reminders to be careful.

Most powerful tools can cause tremendous damage if used recklessly, and the cloud is no exception.

In every industry, there are players seizing the potential of the cloud and upending the old institutions that once seemed immune to competitive threats. In the short term, it may feel easier to ignore the world changing around us and seek comfort in the warm glow of big servers in big rooms with big price tags. But that decision may erode the competitiveness of our businesses to the point of no return. The time is now to decide whether our companies will be bold and join the disruptors or continue to avoid the cloud and hope the status quo will somehow keep us competitive!

The decisions we make today about our technology infrastructure will have a greater impact on the future competitiveness of our businesses than they ever have before.

But before we move on to technologies beyond the cloud, we need to address a dangerous falsehood being promoted as cloud by certain technology companies that will slap a fancy label on anything that will drive sales. We must learn to distinguish clever marketing from real innovation, especially when it comes to the hype that currently surrounds the cloud.

> **WARNING! THE PRIVATE CLOUD IS NOT A REAL THING!**

Free lunch. Unicorns. Automatic faucets that work.

None of these exist.

Neither does the private cloud. The private cloud is intended to mimic the public cloud, but it resides within customers' data centers, whether truly on premises or in shared colocated data centers.

....

The so-called private cloud provides interface mechanisms similar to the public cloud but none of the actual benefits of the (real) public cloud.

....

The private cloud is sold as the best of both worlds. It claims to give the customer all the control they desire with most of the benefits of the public cloud.

These claims are simply untrue.

Let's break it down.

POWER—NO!

The private cloud implies that the computing hardware is owned or fully leased and resident in a customer data center. The customer has access to the purchased power, no more and no less, the way it already is in a fully on-premises solution.

COST—NO!

The private cloud requires the same high-cost structures of on-premises solutions, because it is an on-premises solution. Customers may even need more personnel because of the added overhead to support the cloud like interfaces.

SCALABILITY—NO!

Private cloud customers have access to the hardware they have. If they want more, they need to procure more, find data center space, wire the racks, install the hardware, provision access, ensure security, etc.

SECURITY—NO!

Private cloud customers control their own fate. In a world where thousands of organizations fall victim to ransomware on a long-ago deprecated operating system, doing security is not a core competency for most organizations.

FLEXIBILITY—NO!

The private cloud provides some flexible behavior on the microscale, so long as the capabilities have already been built previously, the computing capacity exists, and the interface to those capabilities has been sufficiently developed. But this is "fake" flexibility: building and paying for excess capacity in order to have the illusion of flexibility is not actual flexibility. It is inefficiency posing as flexibility.

SPEED TO DELIVERY—NO!

The private cloud has none of the above benefits of the public cloud and therefore drives no actual speed to delivery. Failing fast, rapid iteration, trying out the new tools that didn't even exist yesterday—none of these are truly possible in the private cloud.

The only rational conclusion to this analysis is that the private cloud is not the cloud at all. The private cloud is a repackaging of the old ways with new terminology, promoted by legacy organizations that are trying to keep their cash cows relevant long past when the steaks should have been served. Do not fall prey to this clever marketing.

> **We should never use the private cloud as a proof of concept of whether to move to the public cloud. Those who do learn nothing about the benefits of the public cloud, because the private cloud provides none of those benefits.**

HYBRID CLOUD

The private cloud is not a real thing, but the hybrid cloud is.

This is, in effect, cloud technology coming full circle. In the past, because there was no other viable option, we used nearby data centers, whether owned by our organizations or shared spaces owned by somebody else. Now with the cloud, we can tap into better economies of scale in massive, shared environments that may not be across the street.

But what happens when internet access is shaky, or we have a unique use case where it makes more sense to batch upload to the cloud at certain times? What if we have machines which create exabytes of data and it would take years to upload it all?

What about an offshore oil rig? Internet access is likely slow or nonexistent entirely, and yet the operation of the rig generates a tremendous amount of data that would be useful to the parent organization. In normal business, however, the analytics needs of the rig operators likely rely most on the data that is generated locally on the rig. It wouldn't make a lot of sense to upload everything to the cloud first, would it?

How about a passenger jetliner? During every flight, the sensors embedded throughout the plane generate a lot of usage, performance, and maintenance-related data that will help analysts improve airline operations. Most of this is not particularly actionable during the flight itself. Would it make a lot of sense to try to upload via the shaky internet access planes have, or would it be more effective to wait until landing and upload everything in a fraction of the time?

Offshore oil rigs and jetliners are classic examples of the need for hybrid cloud architectures. Technologies available today are well suited to accommodating these use cases and illustrate that when it comes to data, no size fits all. When developing an approach to creating data value, what seems to work most of the time may not be the right solution for our situation.

SERVERLESS AND EVENT-DRIVEN TECHNOLOGIES

The original cloud platforms focused on storage and virtualized servers, and this was good. Everybody had applications that needed to run on servers, and everybody had files that they needed to store. The benefits of the public cloud allowed organizations to move everything into the cloud with manageable amounts of revision.

As time has gone on and the systems have matured, the public cloud has enabled more granular building blocks to emerge along with managed services that take away many of the low-value tasks and tuning from the end consumer so they can focus on the higher-value design and development tasks. Databases, server clusters, web hosting, I/O throughput are just a few examples of what can be changed with a few clicks or even automatically based on utilization.

We have now reached the logical limit of this evolution, where discrete code snippets are executed in response to individual events, all on computing capacity that exists only long enough to execute the code.

To understand what this means, imagine a picture is uploaded to our website, and when that happens, we want to store the photo's storage location and other metadata in a searchable NoSQL database so it can be quickly retrieved on demand. How would we build this functionality in a traditional environment?

We would have a storage array of some sort, along with at least one server sitting ready to process anything that comes in and then log the information to a database that is sitting on at least one other server. This would work fine for a small or predictable throughput of files being uploaded, though to provide sufficient headroom, excess capacity would need to be allocated.

What if we needed to process bursts of an unknown number of files at any time, from one to ten million? In a traditional architecture, we would need a lot more usually idle machinery to accommodate the processing peaks. This is where serverless technologies shine brightest, for obvious reasons.

In a serverless, event-driven world, it does not matter what the throughput looks like, since processing power is allocated automatically when an event is triggered. In our example, this would instantly shift the processing bottleneck to the database, and if it were a managed database, it could identify the utilization spike and grow capacity to accommodate the burst of calls, and then when things settle down, it could shrink its throughput pipes back to a normal level. No 3:00 a.m. phone call required.

The economic impacts of perfectly elastic computing demand are awesome. This has already changed the world, and this is only the beginning! And if we ever find ourselves wondering why Netflix rarely slows down on a Saturday night when demand is spiking, now we might have a better understanding.

OPEN-SOURCE SOFTWARE, PYTHON, AND R

This section is not really about these specific tools. It is really about the democratization of application logic. Coming off the excitement of the cloud section, this is a fascinating complement. It comes down to this.

Almost nothing we create with software is truly new. Somebody has done something like it already. Open-source software exists to address this fact. Nothing we are trying to do is really all that unique from a technical perspective. Why not spend less time reinventing wheels and more time designing new vehicles? Why not build collectively while still retaining the opportunity to capitalize on what makes our businesses truly unique?

Somewhere, the code already *mostly* exists to solve *most* of our challenge.

Just like a traditional encyclopedia writer could never keep pace with Wikipedia, proprietary software development is losing ground to open-source software. Think back to agile—we need to be flexible, fast, and deliberate in our priorities.

Python and R have become de facto standards for application development and deeper data science analysis, respectively. These play nicely in the open-source space and in Linux environments especially. If we are data technology proficient and want to expand our skills with a new language or skill set, a good place to start is Python and R.

So why are these in the same section as open-source software? It's because Python and R follow an open-source model of facilitating sharing and reuse. Not unlike Linux itself, Python makes it easy to bring in external libraries with minimal code. The most common libraries are centrally maintained, giving programmers incredible extensibility without needing to reinvent the wheel every time.

Who knows? In the coming years, Python and R may fall out of favor, but the open-source movement is likely here to stay. The power of the community is too formidable for us to return to the old days of closed, proprietary commodity technology systems. It is simply not possible for those kinds of models to keep up anymore.

INTERNET OF THINGS

IoT has been the next hot new thing for a while. The early days were a bit misguided, thinking that things like Twitter-enabled refrigerators would be the killer applications. That one was a bit off the mark, but we have recently seen an explosion of smart home devices like thermostats, security cameras, lighting, and smoke detectors.

Sensors are the IoT killer app. From the home improvement projects favored by nerds like me to large-scale manufacturing and logistics sensor arrays favored by nerds like General Electric, the ability to measure fine details at massive scale has revolutionary implications.

These days, we are really starting to see the data value side of IoT! Amazon opened the first grocery stores that have no checkout counters, and now someday in the future, people will ask, "What's a checkout counter?" A myriad of systems come together to drive a concept as simple as not making people waste time in a pointless line just waiting to hand over their money.

The kinds of technologies that enable simple sensory functions in individual devices can be combined to do science fiction–like magic. Driverless cars, drones, rockets that fly to space and come back to earth to land upright, the AI sisters (Alexa, Siri, and the Google one), and we are still in the early days!

IoT is where the incredible abilities we have built in the virtual world of computers reach the physical world of people. Previous attempts were hampered by technology limitations, but now it is on, and in a tremendous way. If you have an ability to get involved in it, consider it.

DATA LAKES

Data lakes are a data storage and access layer that can accommodate effectively unlimited scale and complexity, combined with a reasonable amount of structure and context. They are a big part of the reason why big data is no longer a big deal.

By tracking the metadata of data lake objects, we enable new design and development patterns, like decoupling data refinement from data use. In the past, data would be loaded into a data warehouse and would progress through several steps: landing staging production history is a popular progression, but some may add change data capture, master data, data quality, or other similar steps.

With data lakes, we are not required to do these steps in the same database or even at all! We can create derivatives from our source data, write them back to the data lake, and then use those refined versions as the jumping-off point for a multitude of downstream use cases.

This lets us use technologies perfectly suited to the tasks at hand. After all, the specific operations involved in assessing data quality and establishing master data are different from the aggregation mechanisms needed for large-scale reporting and analytics. Once we understand the dynamics of a data lake, it almost seems silly to manage data for analytics in any other way.

> **Whenever we use data, ideally two things happen: First, we do something that creates data value. Second, we create data artifacts from the use. The more we use data, the more data we get!**

What can expand the value of data lakes is recursive loops. This means bringing outputs from a system back into the system. In our context, it means that when we analyze data from a data lake, we can bring the results back into the data lake itself.

Data lakes should track usage artifacts and bring them into the data lake. Context tools can keep everything organized, allowing folks to come along and use the data from other processes without putting the energy in to rerun the same processes again. This amplifies potential ROI from data efforts and helps ensure consistency in downstream artifacts. Recursive loops are extremely powerful amplifiers!

KNOWLEDGE GRAPHS

Graph databases are data repositories that focus on the relationships between data as much as the data itself. Why these are called "graph instead of relational is simply" because the legacy relational databases already claimed the term, even though codifying the relations between data entities is one of the things that relational databases do quite poorly. Relational databases are, however, great at aggregating and calculating numbers with a bunch of other numbers. Sorry, this is confusing, but how these names evolved is an unfortunate circumstance we can't control. Please don't blame the messenger!

Graph databases are built from a foundation of "triples." An overly simplistic description is triples contain a starting entity, an ending entity, and a relationship between them. The triple can have additional properties, bidirectional relationships, self-referencing relationships, and a whole bunch of other structures depending on the specific technology. Our goal here is not to help you understand what triples are but mostly to explain that triples exist and you might want to go learn more about them.

Triple stores allow graph databases to create a visual interface for exploration of relationships alongside data. Even more exciting, if we enrich the data with increasing amounts of insights and harmonization, we can create *knowledge graphs*. Knowledge graphs are built to clearly define the many relationships between entities. If you think of entities as objects or nouns, then the relationships explain how they connect.

If I had a dog, for example, both me and my puppy could be objects in a graph, and a relationship line from me to the dog could say "feeds," and a bidirectional line could say "best friends." Isn't that adorable? It can also be super useful!

....

Knowledge graphs connect what we know about topics across multiple sources, enabling insights beyond what we would learn from individual sources on their own.

....

The pharmaceutical industry is one area where knowledge graphs are impacting how work gets done. Scientists can more easily leverage the work of other scientists to make connections leading to the discovery of new drugs. Because the drug discovery and development processes are so complex, knowledge graphs help whittle away the less important data while helping scientists focus on the best opportunities for additional evaluation.

Knowledge graphs are now starting to take hold more broadly, and the applications are sure to increase further as time goes on.

DATA CATALOGS

Data catalogs are fundamentally metadata repositories with some collaboration and governance functions thrown in. They profile data repositories, capturing all the relevant technical metadata, and do a fair job of describing data movements between systems. Most also contain places to capture business metadata and store information about who owns which data and systems and where to go for more help.

Most have some data lineage functionality but often lack stand-alone data lineage tools in terms of graphical interface design and ease of use. Data catalogs may also facilitate some data governance functions or provide data quality and master data functions.

> **What makes data catalogs appealing is they do so much, reasonably well. What makes data catalogs underwhelming is they are rarely the best solution by themselves for any individual discipline.**

Part of the reason for this is that data catalogs have not quite embraced the graph database technologies we covered in the previous section. It's baffling that most data catalog vendors continue to build their solutions on antiquated relational database technologies when there is clearly a better way. Maybe if they focused on delivering valuable insights and impacts to their users, they'd realize that sometimes we don't need a dictionary; sometimes we need an encyclopedia, or even better, an immediate correct answer to the specific question we have at any moment.

While first we focused on data catalogs as a tool, since that's how most readers will think of them, there's a bigger issue at play.

The real problem is that we've split the atom of data quality. What are typically thought of as discrete functions (lineage, metadata, master data, data quality itself) are all parts of the suitability-of-use story of data.

It's okay that the tools are a bit separate, as the functions are clearly different. But if we think we can "do" data quality without data lineage, for example, we're kidding ourselves again.

Since we begrudgingly acknowledged big data earlier, we now can consider a big data quality level as well! If normal-size data quality is "Is this data suitable for how I want to use it?," big data quality is "Which data is the best for what I want to do?" A subtle but important distinction. We have gone from choosing first and then analyzing to evaluating all the data and then choosing which we should use! This reduces selection bias and errors and improves everything we would do downstream.

TOOLS AND TECHNOLOGY ARE GREAT AMPLIFIERS, BUT BUSINESS IMPACTS MATTER MOST

This chapter has covered a relatively few of the major innovations that data leaders must consider as we embark on our data leadership journey, and there are so many more to come. Although the timeliness of these observations will lessen, history will judge their relevancy. If things like the public cloud and microservices do not stand the test of time, it will be as shocking as if relational databases ever went away. I won't say it is impossible, but I will say it is highly unlikely!

....

Learning more about the innovation trends that will impact us for many years is one of the best ways for data leaders to ensure our own relevancy in the future.

....

In data leadership and simply leadership in general, so much of what we do is about developing a vision for the future and subsequently making it happen. We've already covered so many levels of this fundamental pattern, and we have just one topic left, and it is the final piece in making a true lasting impact on our organizations. And it starts with rethinking one of the most reviled parts of working in an office setting: projects for everything.

CITATION

1 Daniel Newman, "Blockchain 101: How This Next Big Service Will Change the Future," *Forbes*, April 13, 2017, https://www.forbes.com/sites/danielnewman/2017/04/13/blockchain-101-how-this-next-big-service-will-change-the-future/.

15

HARNESS THE TRUE POWER OF DATA

COMPELLED TO MAKE IT BETTER

It's easy to think about projects, since they have definable beginnings and ends along with reasonably clear objectives and expectations. The concept of data projects is appealing but may also oversimplify what we are really trying to accomplish. On one hand, data projects are familiar coordination mechanisms that align behaviors of diverse groups of stakeholders toward a common positive outcome. On the other hand, they are finite, and frequently project sponsors mistakenly believe that when the projects are done, the data value story is complete.

One problem is that data, for better or worse, is often associated with technology, and technology projects often result in something that people can use indefinitely once built, like a software application or a new server coming online.

Data project sponsors may assume that data works similarly, but data is far from a build-it-and-then-we're-done type of effort. Of course, we will never be done with data! This should be obvious by now when we consider things like social media, the IoT, big data, and the fact that even grandmothers have cell phones.

We need to help our organizations understand that these are just the early days before the real insanity to come, and if we are not ready to commit to data excellence for the long term, we are going to be in big trouble. The disruption that we are helping to cause in every industry is changing the way business gets done, and this will not stop any time soon. And if we want to convince people to change their ways, nothing beats a good story.

Let's assume we have a data initiative in mind that will create some amount of data value in our company. What do we do? We might think the first step is to get formal approval to do the project.

The problem is that a project means significant effort, which means providing an assessment of resource requirements, ROI, and opportunity costs. That means we would need to know all those things. If we're just getting going, we simply won't know enough detail to be persuasive with this kind of approach.

We will certainly need to get somebody's permission to get resources for a larger-scale project at some point, but there is a better way. Before attempting to formalize a larger effort, we should first establish credibility and create some initial momentum that we can build on.

....

We need to first demonstrate a nominal amount of real data value before we will convince executives to open the checkbook.

....

The following story is real, and it reinforces one of the most important lessons of this book: that we need to stop talking about data and start making an impact. Some of the minor details have been adjusted to protect folks' privacy, but the main points really happened.

SHOW AND NOT (JUST) TELL: THE EIGHT-SECOND PROOF OF CONCEPT

Several years ago, I was on a consulting engagement with a significantly sized public sector transportation organization that wanted to do more with data analytics. They had rolled out a new fare collection system in the prior few years, and with the new fare system came a wealth of data that the organization hadn't previously seen.

Unfortunately, the vendor of that system had control of all the data, and the vendor provided my client access to this data via a web-based business intelligence tool that could create reports on demand. The fare system collected information on roughly a million rides per day, split between bus and rail services, and a typical report would be a look at total daily ride counts for each of those categories over the course of a month. This is a simple report with a total of sixty numbers (thirty days x two numbers/day).

In the legacy reporting system, this simple report would take forty-two minutes to run but would fail 60 percent of the time. Abysmal, by any modern standard. It seemed the vendor was running this business intelligence environment in the same database where many other core operational tasks were taking place (a big no-no). This poor performance was consistent throughout the data environment, and earlier attempts at data replication and direct access had not resulted in any meaningful improvements.

My team had been invited by the client to help solve their data analytics challenges, and we quickly determined that with this reporting environment, it would be impossible to achieve our goals. The real problem we now faced was figuring out what to do about it.

The IT organization thought everything was fine (!), so they were not particularly interested in adding to their already-overwhelming workload to address the problem. The organization did not have the funds or other resources to go purchase new hardware and put a reengineered, more robust solution in place.

We concluded that our first mission was to find a highly capable, nearly free data analytics technology that could be implemented without any significant assistance from IT. This admittedly seemed unrealistic, but I've always been more stubborn than sensible. Plus, it couldn't hurt to try!

I had heard a bit about public cloud technologies at that point but had not worked much with them outside an underpowered development environment at a prior firm. In our current circumstances, however, it seemed that the cloud might be our best hope to meet our seemingly impossible objectives. After researching options around available technologies, the team decided to do a proof of concept with Amazon Redshift, their petabyte-scale cloud data warehouse solution.

Thank goodness that somebody had the foresight to put in the fare system vendor contract that "data must be delivered from the fare system vendor to our client upon request." So in collaboration with our client, we requested all the data.

If you ever want to see software vendors lose their minds, ask them for *all* the data. It will go something like this:

Us: We would like all the data.
Vendor: How quickly do you need it?
Us: As soon as possible. Ideally today.
Vendor: Which data do you need?
Us: All the data.
Vendor: But what time frame?
Us: All the time frames.
Vendor: Which data points are you looking for?
Us: All the data points.
Vendor: But we can't give you all the data.
Us: We need all the data. Would you like a copy of the contract?
Vendor: We will call you back.

This conversation will happen a few times before they get it, but eventually they will realize that providing the data is what they must ultimately do to get us to stop calling. This is what they get for hoarding all the data in the first place.

In our story, the vendor eventually acquiesced, and we began compiling a series of data extracts that would comprise the billion-plus records that we needed to recreate the database in Amazon Redshift. In total, it took about a month to compile enough data to do a true apples-to-apples comparison between the legacy system and the new one.

Recall that in the legacy system, running our sample report showing a daily breakdown of bus and train rides for a month took forty-two minutes, and it failed 60 percent of the time.

In the new one, the same query hitting a comparable database took just eight seconds and worked every time! Realizing what we'd done, I promptly arranged to meet with the president of the organization, who was the driving force behind our data improvement efforts. He needed to see this.

At the meeting, we explained the challenges of getting data from the legacy environment and what we did to work around it. We explained how with their legacy tool set, it would be impossible to create the high-performing data analytics they desired. We explained that accepting poor performance in one area had made it impossible to make progress in another. And we explained that we'd found a path to fixing it all.

But the most important thing we did was demonstrate it. Instead of talking about how a new technology would help solve their challenges, we said two of the most powerful words we can say to someone we want on our side:

"Watch this."

Eight seconds later, the president of the organization gave a puzzled glance at the other executive who had brought us in to help them and then turned back to me for a moment. He paused, looked me in the eyes, and said, "You can do whatever you want."

It felt almost like he had never seen someone demonstrate value as part of their request. And our request was so modest (please let us keep going down this path!) compared to the kinds of requests a large transit agency president would typically get. Even for those big requests, most of the time, people in his position simply get a nice story with a big ask at the end:

"If we make this purchase, everything will be amazing!"

"If we do this million-dollar project, everything will be amazing!"

"If we can go back to the drawing board, everything will be amazing!"

Instead, we took the initiative to test our hypothesis that this solution might work, and then we shared the data we collected in that testing along with the story we told to make it meaningful to someone with a higher-level frame of reference. Sure, we may have had to build much of it at the coffee shop across the street from the office because the domain was blocked from the network, but we got the data we needed, and those eight seconds made our point better than our best presentation deck.

The key to gaining buy-in is *show*, not just *tell*. This is a philosophy that we as data leaders should try to adopt in everything we do.

People are tired of being let down by well-intended promises that go unfulfilled. If we can give them *real evidence* that what they are hearing from us will be more than that, we are much more likely to get what we seek, whether it is permission, time, money, people, political support, etc.

This lesson also applies to the project management methodologies we deploy once we have permission to proceed. For decades, complex endeavors like data warehouses were built using traditional project management methodologies. Unfortunately, more than half of data warehouse projects fail. Too bad this isn't baseball, where we can make the hall of fame despite failing two-thirds of the time.

If we want to do more than get approval and really deliver on our promises, we need to put it all together from beginning to end.

....

While the DLF outlines the journey of data from potential to real value, transforming our organizations requires everyone to go through their own metamorphosis.

....

TODAY IS AN INFLECTION POINT

Throughout this book, we have asked a lot of questions and provided many *partial* answers. The sad truth is that nobody (not even a consultant!) will have the complete solutions for any given organization until the specific challenges and full contexts are known. But what we do have now is a good start, with some lighthouses to help us navigate our way.

Our goal was to understand the big brushstrokes of what makes realizing data value so difficult yet such a worthwhile pursuit. Data truly represents the future success of all businesses, and those of us who can help lead the way will impact the destiny of our organizations more than we could have ever imagined.

....

Regardless of our specific role today, whether as a junior data analyst trying to build a career or as a senior leader trying to make our organization more competitive in its industry, data value and data leadership are crucial to our future success.

....

By using the coordination tools we discussed throughout this book along with continued study and supplementing our own personal skills with a diverse team, we will continue creating this new, data-driven reality. The one thing we know is that we have no idea what is around the corner. Maybe we can project the next couple of years, but in general, people do not have a great track record in predicting where technology improvements will lead us in the longer term.

There are certainly parallels between today's data revolution with the Industrial Revolution. The nature of people's jobs is changing, and there is a sense of incredible potential and unlimited risk that permeates today's business climate.

None of this really matters.

People do not experience macroeconomics firsthand. It is an aggregation, an abstraction, from the daily reality we each face. Nobody can really change the world by themselves. All we can do is change the individual circumstances of those we impact, and some people can impact more people than others. The president of the United States, typically regarded as the most powerful person in the world, only achieves that power through the cascading influence on those whom he or she can impact.

So why are we talking about this? Why does this matter?

Everything we can accomplish as data leaders is realized through the actions of others.

The structure of projects, getting approvals, showing, not (just) telling—these are likely useful insights (if I do say so myself), but the point is that none of them are terribly important by themselves. Remember the definition of data value.

Our ability to create meaningful outcomes is the one thing that matters, even though the tools and techniques in our repertoires will have a cascading impact on the eventual outcomes we are able to drive. But if we as data leaders can put the knowledge in these pages to use, we will save our companies and build the future we are just beginning to see in focus.

Once upon a time, businesses could be successful without being data driven. Today, shockingly, many outstanding businesses still seemingly thrive without fully embracing data. Some think they have embraced it, but a lack of something as fundamental as organized data governance quickly betrays that belief. They may go through the motions of being data driven but realize little data value.

From my experience, these organizations still represent most businesses out there. We are surrounded by gold, and everybody can see it sitting there, but data leaders are the only ones with the keys to open the doors that will let us bring that value inside.

Data is getting a lot of attention right now, and some of the technology innovations seem impossible. When SpaceX first landed a booster rocket upright on a floating barge, the video looked like bad special effects. Cars are driving themselves more and more, with full autonomy finally within plausible reach.

Data enables truly amazing things, but at the same time, our internet still seems to go out three times a day. The CFO is still complaining that the numbers on her reports do not match. We still cannot quite tell which of our employees are the most productive or which customers contribute the most profit.

The headlines about rockets and self-driving cars capture our attention, but they are the outliers. The norm is that we are still struggling to fully unlock the potential of data in our organizations, and data leaders are the key. We data leaders understand the potential value contained in our data, the many activities necessary to turn that potential into realized value, and the balance required to maximize those real outcomes. Further, we know that understanding these concepts is not enough.

We must take action if we want our businesses to evolve. This is the core of data value, and the role of data leaders is to catalyze these organizational changes.

Data leadership is not a role for the timid. Data by itself is challenging enough—technically difficult to master and even more arduous to talk about. Leadership is just as tough. It is not easy to get people united behind a common goal, working together to achieve extraordinary outcomes.

When we consider that everyone we work with goes home to an entire world that exists outside the office, it is amazing that we can gain their attention long enough to make successful businesses. Sometimes it goes sideways. After all, who hasn't had a workday dominated by personal issues? Sick kids, house problems, car trouble. Life has a way of interfering with work from time to time.

But through it all, our lives depend on others' work. As consumers, don't we want data-driven businesses serving us? Phone support that doesn't leave us on hold? Deliveries that show up on time? Emergency services that can get to us quickly?

Data leadership is the glue that connects data and people. It leads to the goods and services we all rely on every day. Data leadership is how it all comes together to create businesses that will use data to better serve each one of us: at the office, at home, and everywhere else.

This book has started us on our data leadership journey, but it's just the beginning. We should remember the definition of data value and orient everything we do to creating more of it. Learn from every opportunity, and try to get a little better at something every day. Find the balance that data leadership enables, and let nothing stop us from overcoming any challenge that stands in our way.

Finally, try to enjoy it. Being a data leader is among the best careers in the world.

Go make an impact!

ACKNOWLEDGMENTS

When I set out on the mission to create a data leadership book, I knew I had to do something different. As much as I admire (and envy) the serious data books out there, they often fail to reflect the dynamic personalities of their authors. And as much as I've long been inspired by great leadership books, it can be difficult to connect their big picture strategies to the day-to-day jobs in which most of us operate. My hope with this book is to give everyone, from CEOs to frontline staff, an entertaining read with enough data leadership strategy and tactical guidance to create real benefits for their organizations.

I'd like to think we succeeded, and I know I couldn't have done it alone. While some of the following folks were directly involved in the production of this book, others in the production of my career, and others in the production of me, you all played a big part and I will never be able to thank you enough.

To my editor, Anna Michels, thank you so much for helping mold my words into something humans can understand! It has been an absolute pleasure working with you throughout this process. I am in awe of how you do what you do.

To the entire Sourcebooks organization, thank you for the opportunity and all your efforts in bringing this book to the world beyond the data management community. After all, a book chock full of amazing data knowledge, hilarious data jokes, and riveting data stories—but lacking readers—doesn't create much value. Kind of like data itself!

To Heather Hall, thank you for sharing your wisdom and introducing me to Sourcebooks. Your passion for books is comparable to my passion for data leadership, and it has been an honor to spend a little time living in your world.

To the DATAVERSITY organization, with special thanks to Tony Shaw, Shannon Kempe, and Charles Roe. You have been such consistent partners for so long and have given me countless opportunities to build and hone my craft. There is no limit to my appreciation for what you've done for me, personally, and the entire data management community.

To Bob Seiner, over the years you have become a friend and mentor, in descending order (and you are an amazing mentor). Thank you for so, so many great conversations and guidance on, well, everything.

To Kasu Sista, I imagine I would have found this data world eventually, but you certainly found me. Thank you for bringing me under your wing and teaching me to fly. I am so grateful for your support at every stage.

To Dorothy Tully, thank you for lending your unique talent in creating delightful illustrations for this book. My words alone could never make the same impact.

To Jane Howard, thank you for the advice and support

throughout my life. Your entrepreneurial lessons are insightful, but your unwavering kindness inspires me most.

To Helen, Arthur, Irene, and Elaine, you are the center of my world. Thank you for your understanding and support when I prioritize work even though I'd rather spend time with you. Your confidence gives me confidence and makes me believe that together we can accomplish anything.

To Mom, you gave me the courage to pursue any crazy idea (and I had many!). You let me make some great mistakes, learning important lessons, but always in a safe way. As I get older, seeing my own children grow, I appreciate how extraordinarily you prepared me for my life. Thank you for all of it (especially the drum set!).

To Allison and Chris, you are wonderful siblings I know I can count on at any time. Though we are all off in our own families now, we'll always share experiences no one else has had. I'm inspired by the paths you are following, and I thank you for always being there throughout life's ups and downs.

To my oldest and dearest friends, Brian Manion, Brian Coyle, Lauren Macey, and Jason Hlavacs, you have been there through it all. And you stuck around. None of us particularly deserves to have this kind of enduring friendship that so few have, but I know how much we all appreciate it. I can't imagine me being me without you. Thank you for being a source of strength and laughter throughout our many adventures over the decades.

To my data management colleagues, who have been beacons of light guiding my career. Each of you has taught and inspired me, and I am so thankful for being welcomed into your world: John Ladley, Peter Aiken, Len Silverston, William Tanenbaum, April Reeve, Danette McGilvray, Scott Taylor, Doug Laney, Thomas Redman, Malcolm Hawker, Kelle O'Neal, Malcolm

Chisholm, Davida Berger, Frank Cerwin, Catherine Nolan, George Yuhasz, and Michael Miller.

To others from whom I learned a tremendous amount, both professionally and personally. Thank you for sharing a part of your journey with me: Stuart Anderson, Lisa Takata, Brian Martin, Andrell Holloway, Garrett Vandendries, Rob Hinds, Rachel Lawrence, Yesenia Echevarria, Matt Rager, Casey Bass, Rozilyn Dupiton, Kate Wharton, Jason Pirtle, Ross Buck, Corey Vest, Will Wangles, Andranik Khatchatrian, Dave Gaddy, K. Sean Frey, Rish Dua, Andrew Smith, Dominic Conenna, Kevin O'Grady, Adam Dillman, Leonard Sagalov, Joseph Dennis, Andrew Giordano, Jeff Block, Joe DeCosmo, Evan Terry, Jules Clement, John Nogle, Harry Kraemer, Steven Rogers, Andrew Lang, Karl Janowski, Ken Frazier, Dan Hibel, Christopher Abtahi, Marty Lefty, Dan Burras, David Claudon, Fred Hoyt, Bob Lombardi, Warren Kistner, and Malinda Carlson. I could easily triple this list, and it is beyond humbling to think about all the amazing people whose paths have crossed with my own.

To the organizations that gave me the career experiences to write this book: Morningstar, Stein Roe Investment Counsel, REFCO, Ronin Capital, West Monroe Partners, RGP, Chicago Transit Authority, Uturn Data Solutions, AbbVie, and all the other colleagues and clients I've worked alongside throughout my career. Many of you will never realize how much our time together means to me. Thank you for it all.

If I've overlooked anyone, I'm sincerely sorry. I'll never do justice to the gratitude I feel to the countless people from whom I've learned, and attempting to contain it within a short acknowledgments section seems to be an exercise in futility.

INDEX

B

back-end integration specialists, 113

baseball acquisition, 59–63

behavioral change, 63–67, 76

benchmarks, 11, 109

best practices versus best of breed, x–xi

big data, 122, 254–256

big data quality, 276

blockchain, 254

blocks to progress, 65

brainstorming, 141–142

Burke, Chris, 61–63, 215–216

business data as high-data value density, 122–123

business glossaries, 123

business/IT relationship

  addressing conflict in, 26–31

  chief digital officer role and, 234–236

  data leadership as business leadership, 230–231, 238–239

  dysfunctionality in, 22–26

  overview, 15–19

  self-interest and, 31–34

  as team, 20–21, 203

business operations, 163–169, 225–226, 286–287

business requirements, use of term, 18

business strategy

  compliance and, 91

  data strategy and, 192–197

  experts in on leadership team, 222

  underinvestment in, 236

C

catalogs, data, 275–276

certainty, waiting for, 142–143

change

  behavioral change, 63–67, 76

  data leadership framework and, 197–199

  organizational change, 75

  resistance to, 174, 200, 204, 225

  in technology, 4–6

cherry picking data, 219

chief analysis officer (CAO), 231–237

chief data officer (CDO), 231–237, 238

chief digital officer (CDO), 231–237

chief information officers (CIOs), 29–31, 236, 237–239

chief information security officers (CISOs), 30, 92–93

chief technology officers (CTOs), 236

Microsoft Excel, 185–186

mistakes, 142–143, 152

modeling, 146–153

momentum

   adoption and, 199–206

   balancing in data leadership framework, 94

   data projects and, 279–285

   importance of, 55–56

   leading by example, 202

   meetings and, 46–47, 55, 59

   resistance to, 217–218

   simple virtuous cycle and, 56–59

   speed up to speed up, 216–220

   team to create and maintain, 221–222

   wrangling and, 110

monetization, 186–189

motivation, 33–34, 205–206

N

NOAA website, 104–105, 138–139

NoSQL, 251

O

open-source software, 269–270

operational systems, architecture and, 95–96, 99

operations, 163–169, 225–226, 286–287

orchestra analogy, 198

organizational change, 225

organizational health, as nebulous, 72–73

outcomes, intentions versus, 54, 59–63

P

partnership, business and IT, 20–21, 203. *See also* business/IT relationship

pay-what-we-use model, 253, 260, 269

people

   inclusion of range of, 225–228

   motivation of, 33–34, 205–206

   resistance to change and, 174, 200, 204, 225

   self-interest and, 31–34, 204–205

   as weak link, 158, 179–180

perfection, pursuit of, 126–127, 129–130, 133, 135

perspectives on data, 140

The Phoenix Project (Kim et al.), 195–196

potential versus realized value, 9, 12–13, 75. *See also* Refine: Build Potential; Use: Deliver Insights

predictive modeling, 177

V

W

ABOUT THE AUTHOR

 Anthony J. Algmin is a data leadership advocate who has led strategic transformations in many industries as a management consultant, data architect, program lead, chief data officer, and entrepreneur. He has performed hundreds of public speaking appearances and is a prolific writer, podcast host, trainer, and adviser to organizations of all sizes. Anthony is known for his passionate, energetic style and letting nothing get in the way of delivering the power of data to those who need it.

Anthony earned a bachelor's degree from Illinois Wesleyan University and an MBA from the Kellogg School of Management. His personal interests include data-forward pursuits like electric vehicles, gaming, auto racing, and other sports. Anthony lives with his wife and three children in suburban Chicago. He would like to get a dog someday. Learn more and connect with Anthony at algmin.com.

ABOUT THE ILLUSTRATOR

Dorothy Tully is a dynamic artist and author who always has an abundance of ideas! She is best known for her upbeat, colorful illustrations of animals and the natural world. She writes and illustrates whimsical children's books, the latest being *Koalabirds*. Dorothy's other passion is sewing, so when not drawing, she creates quilts, bags, and other vibrant one-of-a-kind treasures and designs her own sewing patterns. Dorothy has a BFA in design from Carnegie Mellon University. She lives with her husband, two daughters, two dogs, one cat, and a crazy garden full of fun in Rhode Island. She enjoys blogging about her creative path to inspire others to notice and connect to the joy around us. To see more of her work, please visit her website and online shop www.dorybird.com.